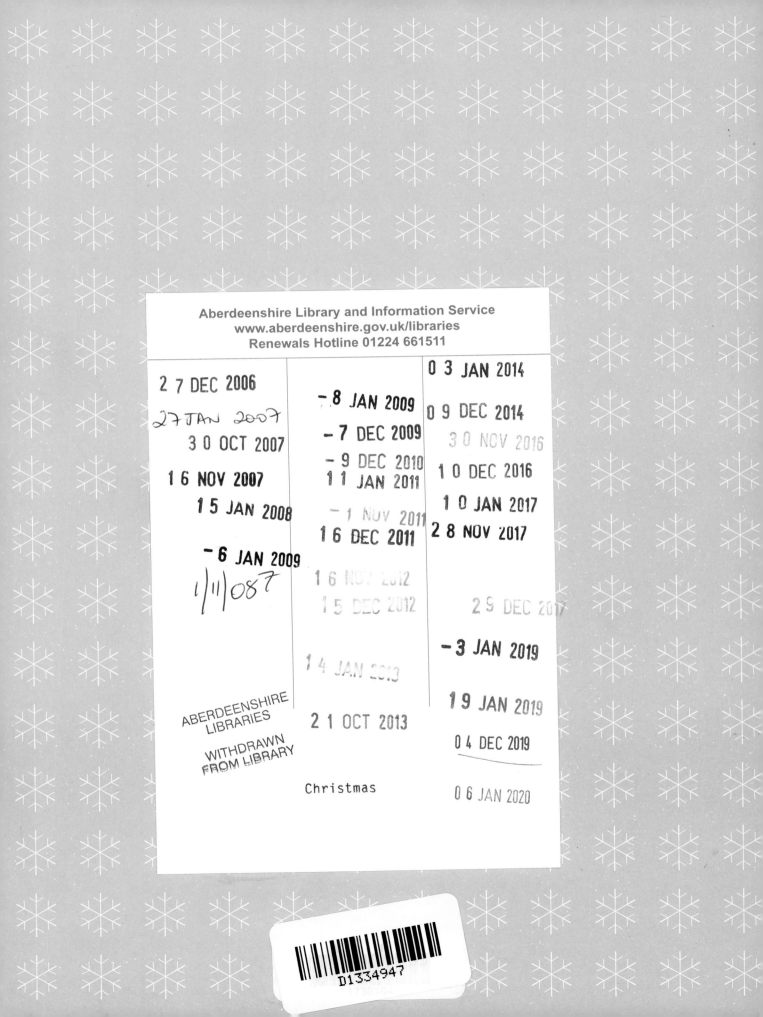

Christmas
FOOD & CRAFT

THE AUSTRALIAN
Women's Weekly

Christmas
FOOD & CRAFT

acp books

contents

season's greetings

The celebration of Christmas is a joyful mix of friends, family, food and festive cheer. From drinks and starters to mains, cakes and desserts, everything you need for a stress-free Christmas is here, including menu suggestions and ideas on table settings, decorations and gift wrapping.

Everything you need for the craft projects is readily available from a variety of stores, including arts and craft, stationery, hobby, wedding supply, homewares and department stores; flowers and foliage for the wreaths are available from local florists. Our ideas are suggestions only; decide on your own colour scheme and make your own creative designs to suit your theme.

Merry Christmas

food

starters

The festive season is a time for celebrating, sharing and relaxing. Great drinks and food are at the top of everyone's wish-list at holiday events and, while waistlines may be a consideration the rest of the year, your guests are happy to indulge themselves during the holidays. Whether entertaining friends or having the family over for a traditional feast, the success of the gathering is just about guaranteed when your starters hit the right note. Mocktails, cocktails and finger food don't need a lot of time or effort to be impressive as well as delicious, and if they seamlessly segue into the first course, there'll be no interruption in the escalating mood of fun and festivity. Here, we share some top ideas for drinks and starters that help to make the season bright.

apple cranberry cosmopolitan

PREPARATION TIME 5 MINUTES SERVES 1

1 cup ice cubes

45ml vodka

30ml Cointreau

10ml cranberry juice

15ml apple juice

5ml lime juice

1 Combine ice cubes, vodka, Cointreau and juices in cocktail shaker; shake vigorously.
2 Strain into chilled 230ml glass. Garnish with 2cm strip apple peel, if desired.

long island iced tea

PREPARATION TIME 5 MINUTES SERVES 1

1 cup ice cubes

30ml vodka

30ml tequila

30ml white rum

30ml gin

15ml Cointreau

15ml lemon juice

15ml sugar syrup (see recipe, page 13)

30ml cola

1 Place ice cubes in 300ml highball glass; add remaining ingredients, stir with swizzle stick.
2 Garnish with a twist of lemon rind and a fresh mint sprig, if desired.

SUGAR SYRUP Stir 1 cup (220g) caster sugar with 1 cup (250ml) water in small saucepan over low heat until sugar dissolves; bring to a boil, simmer, uncovered, without stirring, 5 minutes. Remove from heat; cool to room temperature. Makes about 1½ cups.

lime and mint spritzer

PREPARATION TIME 5 MINUTES SERVES 8

½ cup sugar syrup (see recipe, above)

1 cup (250ml) lime juice

1.25 litres (5 cups) chilled mineral water

¼ cup coarsely chopped fresh mint

1 Combine syrup in large jug with remaining ingredients. Serve immediately, with ice, if desired.

champagne cocktail

PREPARATION TIME 5 MINUTES SERVES 1

Use marginally less than ⅔ cup of Champagne for each cocktail and you will be able to make five cocktails from one bottle of Champagne.

1 sugar cube

5 drops Angostura bitters

⅔ cup (160ml) chilled Champagne

5cm strip orange rind, sliced thinly

1 Place sugar cube in champagne glass; top with bitters then Champagne. Garnish with rind.

mixed berry punch

PREPARATION TIME 15 MINUTES (PLUS REFRIGERATION TIME) SERVES 8

1 teabag

1 cup (250ml) boiling water

120g raspberries

150g blueberries

125g strawberries, halved

¼ cup loosely packed fresh mint leaves

750ml chilled sparkling apple cider

2½ cups (625ml) chilled lemonade

1 Place teabag in mug, cover with the boiling water; stand 10 minutes. Squeeze teabag over mug, discard teabag; cool tea 10 minutes.

2 Using fork, crush raspberries in punch bowl; add blueberries, strawberries, mint and tea. Stir to combine, cover; refrigerate 1 hour. Stir cider and lemonade into punch just before serving.

watermelon refresher

PREPARATION TIME 5 MINUTES MAKES 1 LITRE (4 CUPS)

You need a 1.5kg piece of watermelon for this recipe.

900g seedless watermelon, chopped coarsely

½ cup (125ml) orange juice, chilled

40ml lime juice

1 Blend or process ingredients until smooth.
2 Garnish with lime slices, and serve with ice, if desired.

coffee liqueur eggnog

PREPARATION TIME 10 MINUTES
(PLUS REFRIGERATION TIME) MAKES 1½ LITRES **(6 CUPS)**

While it's traditional to use brandy in eggnog, we used Kahlua, a coffee-flavoured liqueur, in this version.

4 eggs, separated
⅓ cup (75g) caster sugar
2 cups (500ml) hot milk
⅔ cup (160ml) Kahlua
½ cup (125ml) cream

1 Place egg yolks, sugar and milk in large heatproof bowl over a saucepan of simmering water (don't allow water to touch the bottom of the bowl). Whisk about 15 minutes or until mixture lightly coats the back of a metal spoon. Remove from heat, stir in liqueur, cover; refrigerate 1 hour.

2 Beat cream in small bowl until soft peaks form; fold into liqueur mixture.

3 Beat egg whites in small bowl with electric mixer until soft peaks form; gently fold into liqueur mixture, in two batches.

chocolate martini

PREPARATION TIME 5 MINUTES **SERVES** 1

chocolate Ice Magic
45ml vodka
45ml crème de cacao
1 cup ice cubes
20ml Irish cream
10ml framboise

1 Pipe a 12cm-circle with Ice Magic onto a flat plate. Quickly twist the rim of a 150ml cocktail glass in the chocolate; sit glass upright in freezer to set.

2 Meanwhile, combine vodka, crème de cacao and half of the ice cubes in cocktail shaker. Shake vigorously; strain into glass.

3 Combine remaining ice cubes, Irish cream and framboise in shaker. Shake vigorously; pour carefully over back of a spoon into glass so mixture floats on top. Do not stir. Garnish with small chocolate slivers and a fresh raspberry, if desired.

starters ✳ nibbles

three dips

Serve the dips with raw or lightly steamed vegetables, bread sticks or crackers.

pistou (basil dip)

PREPARATION TIME 5 MINUTES MAKES 1 CUP

100g fresh basil leaves

⅔ cup (160ml) olive oil

1 clove garlic, quartered

2 teaspoons finely grated
lemon rind

2 tablespoons finely grated
parmesan

1 Blend or process ingredients until smooth.

TIP Keep, covered, in the refrigerator for up to three days.

tapenade (olive dip)

PREPARATION TIME 10 MINUTES MAKES 1½ CUPS

300g large seeded black olives

2 tablespoons drained capers,
rinsed

1 clove garlic, quartered

2 tablespoons lemon juice

1 tablespoon fresh
flat-leaf parsley leaves

⅓ cup (80ml) olive oil

1 Blend or process ingredients until smooth.

TIP Keep, covered, in the refrigerator for up to one week.

anchovy dip

PREPARATION TIME 5 MINUTES MAKES 1 CUP

40 drained anchovy fillets

1 tablespoon lemon juice

2 cloves garlic, quartered

3 teaspoons fresh
lemon thyme leaves

⅓ cup (80ml) olive oil

2 tablespoons hot water

1 Blend or process anchovies, juice, garlic and thyme until smooth. With motor operating, add oil in a thin, steady stream until mixture thickens. Transfer to bowl; stir in the water.

TIP Keep, covered, in the refrigerator for up to one week.

hints Oysters are fabulous served as one-swallow shooters. Make a pitcher of bloody (or virgin) marys and half fill 24 shot glasses; add a shelled oyster and a sprinkle of finely chopped chives to each. Or try the same shooter idea with a mixture of equal parts V-8 juice and tequila with the addition of a bit of freshly grated horseradish. Oysters are ideally served on a bed of crushed ice, especially in the summer, or nestled on a platter in a bed of rock salt to prevent their sliding around. If you don't want to serve them on the half shell, place single oysters on chinese soup spoons then top them with a little combined lime juice and fish sauce and a sprinkle of finely shredded lime rind and fresh coriander.

vodka-cured gravlax

PREPARATION TIME 10 MINUTES (PLUS REFRIGERATION TIME) **MAKES** 24

1 tablespoon sea salt

1 teaspoon finely ground black pepper

1 tablespoon sugar

1 tablespoon vodka

300g salmon fillet, skin on

24 mini toasts

SOUR CREAM SAUCE

⅓ cup (80g) sour cream

2 teaspoons drained baby capers, rinsed

2 teaspoons lemon juice

2 teaspoons finely chopped drained cornichons

½ small red onion (50g), chopped finely

1 Combine salt, pepper, sugar and vodka in small bowl.

2 Remove bones from fish; place fish, skin-side down, on piece of plastic wrap. Spread vodka mixture over flesh side of fish; enclose securely in plastic wrap. Refrigerate overnight, turning parcel several times.

3 Combine ingredients for sour cream sauce in small bowl.

4 Slice fish thinly; spread sauce on toasts, top with fish.

oysters with two dressings

PREPARATION TIME 5 MINUTES **MAKES** 24

RED WINE VINEGAR DRESSING

1½ teaspoons finely chopped shallots

1 tablespoon red wine vinegar

1 teaspoon extra virgin olive oil

12 oysters, on the half shell

RED WINE VINEGAR DRESSING

1 Combine shallots, vinegar and oil in screw-top jar; shake well.

2 Just before serving, drizzle oysters with dressing.

SPICY LIME DRESSING

1½ tablespoons lime juice

½ teaspoon hot chilli sauce

1 teaspoon finely chopped fresh coriander

12 oysters, on the half shell

SPICY LIME DRESSING

1 Place juice, sauce and coriander in screw-top jar; shake well.

2 Just before serving, drizzle oysters with dressing.

corn fritters with sour cream

PREPARATION TIME 25 MINUTES (PLUS STANDING TIME) **COOKING TIME** 15 MINUTES **MAKES** 35

½ cup (75g) plain flour

½ cup (75g) self-raising flour

2 eggs, beaten lightly

½ cup (125ml) buttermilk

½ teaspoon sugar

420g can corn kernels, drained

2 small zucchini (150g), grated coarsely

2 cloves garlic, crushed

1 small brown onion (80g), chopped finely

8 drained anchovy fillets, chopped finely

¼ cup coarsely chopped fresh flat-leaf parsley

¼ cup (20g) grated parmesan

2 tablespoons olive oil

½ cup (120g) sour cream

½ cup (125ml) sweet chilli sauce

1 Sift flours into large bowl; make a well in the centre. Gradually whisk in eggs, buttermilk and sugar.

2 Stir in corn, zucchini, garlic, onion, anchovies, parsley and cheese. Stand 30 minutes.

3 Heat oil in large frying pan; drop heaped teaspoonfuls of mixture into pan. Cook until browned both sides and cooked through.

4 Serve fritters topped with sour cream and sweet chilli sauce.

TIPS This recipe can be prepared several hours ahead. The fritters are best cooked close to serving.

fig and fetta

PREPARATION TIME 10 MINUTES MAKES 24

125g marinated fetta

1 tablespoon finely chopped fresh chives

24 mini toasts

3 medium fresh figs (180g)

1 Mash cheese with chives in small bowl; spread on toast.

2 Cut each fig into eight wedges; place one wedge on each toast. Sprinkle with coarsely ground black pepper.

barbecued duck and ginger tartlets

PREPARATION TIME 10 MINUTES
COOKING TIME 5 MINUTES MAKES 32

2 cups (320g) shredded chinese barbecued duck meat

32 x 4cm tartlet cases

¼ cup hoisin sauce

2cm piece fresh ginger (10g), grated

2 green onions, sliced thinly

1 Preheat oven to 220°C/200°C fan-forced.

2 Divide meat among tartlet cases.

3 Combine sauce and ginger in screw-top jar; shake well. Divide mixture among tartlets.

4 Heat in oven 5 minutes; serve tartlets topped with onion.

tarragon and lime scallops

PREPARATION TIME 15 MINUTES
COOKING TIME 10 MINUTES MAKES 24

24 scallops, without roe (500g)

2 tablespoons coarsely chopped fresh tarragon

1 tablespoon lime juice

1 tablespoon olive oil

3 limes, each cut into 8 wedges

1 Combine scallops, tarragon, juice and oil in medium bowl.

2 Thread one scallop and one lime wedge on each skewer. Cook, in batches, on heated oiled grill plate (or grill or barbecue) until scallops are cooked.

TIPS You need 24 bamboo skewers for this recipe; soak in cold water for at least an hour prior to use to prevent splintering or scorching. Scallops and lime wedges can be skewered up to an hour ahead. Cover; refrigerate until required.

sticky-glazed pork with pineapple

PREPARATION TIME 10 MINUTES
(PLUS REFRIGERATION TIME)
COOKING TIME 15 MINUTES MAKES 32

2 pork fillets (600g)

2 tablespoons char sui sauce

1 tablespoon light soy sauce

½ small pineapple (450g), sliced thinly

½ cup (25g) snow pea sprouts, trimmed

1 Combine pork and sauces in large bowl. Refrigerate, covered, 1 hour.

2 Cook pineapple on heated oiled grill plate (or grill or barbecue) until browned lightly. Remove from grill, cover to keep warm. Halve slices.

3 Cook pork over low heat on grill plate, covered, about 10 minutes or until cooked. Cover; stand 5 minutes then slice thinly.

4 Top pineapple with 2 slices of pork then sprouts.

hints Take these two ideas for edible "plates" as part of your nibbles presentation and develop them – you'll come up with equally clever and practically limitless other ideas: tiny blini or rösti, polenta squares, upturned mushrooms, baby cos or betel leaves, crisped wonton wrappers or tortilla wedges – and that's just for starters. First plan the topping then think about creating a base for it that relates harmoniously in taste or texture, or one that smacks of the same cuisine. Not only aesthetically pleasing but pragmatically too: less washing up. Plus, these novel little bases are also a yummy platform for showing off your ingenuity as a creative cook.

roast beef with caramelised onion on rye

PREPARATION TIME 20 MINUTES **COOKING TIME** 30 MINUTES **MAKES** 40

500g beef fillet

1 tablespoon olive oil

2 large red onions (600g), sliced thinly

1 tablespoon brown sugar

1 tablespoon red wine vinegar

1 loaf rye bread (660g)

¼ cup (60ml) olive oil, extra

2 tablespoons mild english mustard

⅓ cup finely chopped fresh flat-leaf parsley

1 Preheat oven to 180°C/160°C fan-forced.

2 Cook beef in heated, oiled medium frying pan until browned all over; place in small baking dish. Roast, uncovered, in oven about 20 minutes or until cooked. Wrap beef in foil.

3 Heat oil in same pan; cook onion until soft. Add sugar and vinegar; cook, stirring, until caramelised.

4 Preheat grill. Cut bread into 1.5cm slices; cut each slice into quarters. Brush bread, both sides, with extra oil; toast both sides under grill.

5 Slice beef thinly. Spread mustard on bread; top with beef and onion, sprinkle with parsley.

spicy chicken salad in witlof

PREPARATION TIME 20 MINUTES **COOKING TIME** 15 MINUTES **MAKES** 24

1 tablespoon sesame oil

300g chicken mince

1 tablespoon fish sauce

2 tablespoons lime juice

1 tablespoon palm sugar

1 tablespoon finely chopped vietnamese mint

1 tablespoon finely chopped fresh coriander

4 baby witlof leaves, separated

CORIANDER PASTE

2 coriander roots, chopped coarsely

3 cloves garlic, peeled

2cm piece fresh ginger (10g), grated

10 white peppercorns

1 Using a small blender, spice grinder or mortar and pestle, blend or pound ingredients for coriander paste until smooth.

2 Heat oil in wok, add paste; cook, stirring, until fragrant.

3 Add chicken; cook, stirring, until browned lightly.

4 Add sauce, juice and sugar; simmer, uncovered, 3 minutes or until thickened slightly. Stir in mint and coriander.

5 Divide mixture evenly among witlof leaves.

TIPS Chicken filling can be prepared three hours ahead. Assemble salad close to serving. Recipe can be served either warm or cold.

antipasti

PREPARATION TIME 15 MINUTES COOKING TIME 20 MINUTES SERVES 6

400g piece baked ricotta

⅛ teaspoon smoked paprika

¼ teaspoon dried chilli flakes

¼ teaspoon dried
oregano leaves

250g cherry tomatoes

½ cup (125ml) extra virgin
olive oil

1 medium eggplant (300g),
sliced thinly

2 tablespoons small fresh
basil leaves

3 chorizo (400g), sliced

¼ cup lightly packed fresh
flat-leaf parsley leaves

12 fresh asparagus spears,
trimmed

¼ cup (20g) parmesan flakes

10 trimmed red radishes (150g)

150g marinated seeded
kalamata olives

1 Preheat oven to 180°C/160°C fan-forced.

2 Place ricotta on shallow oven tray; sprinkle with paprika, chilli and oregano. Place tomatoes on same tray. Drizzle ricotta and tomatoes with 2 tablespoons of the oil; roast about 10 minutes or until tomatoes begin to split.

3 Brush eggplant slices with 2 tablespoons of the oil; cook in grill pan (or pan-fry or barbecue) until browned both sides. Drizzle eggplant with another 1 tablespoon of oil; top with basil.

4 Cook chorizo in grill pan (or pan-fry or barbecue) until browned both sides; combine in small bowl with parsley.

5 Cook asparagus in large frying pan of simmering water until just tender; drain. Top asparagus with parmesan; drizzle with remaining oil.

6 Serve ricotta, tomatoes, eggplant, chorizo, asparagus, radishes and olives on large platter.

TIP Asparagus could also be cooked in grill pan (or pan-fried or barbecued) until just tender.

hints Light and lovely does it every time: given a choice, go for glamour over substance with your first course. Your guests have just had a few nibbles, and your pièce de résistance awaits its deserved reception, so don't make this part of the meal too filling. And choose its content so that it relates well with the main, neither echoing nor fighting it. Here, seafood with fruit and the carpaccio are good examples of suitable entrées; each can be played around with and slightly altered to include different ingredients, yet retain the same light touch. Carpaccio can be made with thinly sliced raw fish like tuna, kingfish or ocean trout, and smoked salmon or crisp whitebait can replace the salad's prawns.

prawn, pink grapefruit and fetta salad

PREPARATION TIME 30 MINUTES SERVES 8

24 cooked large prawns (1.5kg)

2 baby cos lettuce

2 pink grapefruit (800g), peeled, segmented

200g fetta, crumbled

CHILLI MINT DRESSING

½ cup (125ml) olive oil

¼ cup (60ml) red wine vinegar

1 teaspoon white sugar

1 fresh long red chilli, sliced thinly

½ cup finely shredded fresh mint

1 Combine ingredients for chilli mint dressing in screw-top jar; shake well.

2 Shell and devein prawns, leaving tails intact.

3 Wash and dry whole lettuce leaves.

4 Serve lettuce, prawns, grapefruit and fetta drizzled with chilli mint dressing.

TIPS This recipe can be prepared three hours ahead. Add mint to dressing just before serving.

beef carpaccio with rocket, parmesan and aïoli

PREPARATION TIME 20 MINUTES (PLUS FREEZING TIME) SERVES 4

Carpaccio is to the Italians as sashimi is to the Japanese. This thinly sliced raw beef fillet is usually served drizzled with olive oil and lemon juice.

400g piece beef fillet, trimmed

80g wild rocket

100g parmesan, shaved

AÏOLI

1 egg

1 clove garlic, quartered

1 tablespoon lemon juice

1 tablespoon dijon mustard

½ cup (125ml) olive oil

1 Wrap beef tightly in plastic; freeze about 1 hour or until partially frozen.

2 Make aïoli.

3 Using sharp knife, slice unwrapped beef as thinly as possible. Arrange beef on serving plate; drizzle with aïoli, top with rocket and cheese.

AÏOLI Blend or process egg, garlic, juice and mustard until combined. With motor operating, add oil in a thin, steady stream until aïoli thickens slightly.

chicken, basil and sun-dried tomato terrine

PREPARATION TIME 20 MINUTES COOKING TIME 1 HOUR (PLUS COOLING AND REFRIGERATION TIME) SERVES 8

600g chicken breast fillets, chopped coarsely

350g chicken thigh fillets, chopped coarsely

300g chicken mince

½ cup (80g) roasted pine nuts

½ cup coarsely chopped fresh basil

½ cup (75g) drained semi-dried tomatoes, chopped coarsely

¼ cup (60ml) cream

CAPSICUM SALSA

1 cup (200g) drained char-grilled capsicum, chopped finely

¼ teaspoon cayenne pepper

1 Preheat oven to 180°C/160°C fan-forced.

2 Oil 1.5-litre (6-cup) terrine dish; line base and two long sides with baking paper, extending paper 3cm above sides.

3 Combine ingredients in large bowl; press mixture into dish, fold sides of baking paper over chicken mixture, cover with foil.

4 Place terrine in baking dish; pour enough boiling water into baking dish to come halfway up side of terrine. Cook about 1 hour or until chicken is cooked. Cool to room temperature; drain away excess liquid. Cover; refrigerate 3 hours or overnight.

5 Combine ingredients for capsicum salsa in small bowl.

6 Serve sliced terrine with capsicum salsa.

hints Combining fruit and meat in a recipe confirms the adage that opposites attract. What might seem the unlikeliest of relationships can, with an innovate cook serving as matchmaker, become a marriage made in culinary heaven. These two recipes both call for fig as the featured fruit, yet melon, mandarin, peach or even pomegranate could serve as delicious foils to either the ham or quail. Don't be hesitant about amending simple compilations like these – it is, after all, Christmas, and indulgence is perfectly allowable. Swap the blue brie for bocconcini and the ham for prosciutto to make our salad Italian; change the quail to barbecued duck and the dish assumes a Chinese guise.

ham, blue brie and figs
with honey mustard dressing

PREPARATION TIME 15 MINUTES **SERVES 4**

1 radicchio lettuce

150g wild rocket

250g thinly sliced leg ham
(or turkey or chicken)

4 medium figs (240g), quartered

115g packet blue brie cheese,
sliced thinly

HONEY MUSTARD DRESSING

1 tablespoon wholegrain
mustard

2 teaspoons honey

⅓ cup (80ml) olive oil

¼ cup (60ml) lemon juice

3 teaspoons white wine vinegar

1 Combine ingredients for honey mustard dressing in screw-top jar;
shake well.

2 Combine radicchio, rocket, ham, figs and brie in large bowl; serve,
drizzled with dressing.

quail, fig and orange salad

PREPARATION TIME 20 MINUTES **COOKING TIME** 20 MINUTES **SERVES 4**

6 quails (1.2kg)

3 medium oranges (720g)

4 medium fresh figs (240g),
quartered

100g mizuna

½ cup (60g) coarsely chopped
roasted pecans

MAPLE ORANGE DRESSING

⅓ cup (80ml) orange juice

¼ cup (60ml) olive oil

2 tablespoons pure maple syrup

1 clove garlic, crushed

1 Combine ingredients for maple orange dressing in screw-top jar;
shake well.

2 Rinse quails under cold water; pat dry. Discard necks from quails.
Using scissors, cut along each side of each quail's backbone; discard
backbones. Halve each quail along breastbone; brush with half the
dressing. Cook quail, uncovered, on heated oiled grill plate until cooked.

3 Segment oranges over large bowl; add remaining ingredients and
dressing, toss gently.

4 Serve salad topped with quails.

mains

Contemporary or traditional, it's your call, but remember that it is the main event, the course most lingered over, that part of a feast linking starter and dessert, the food that most highlights your culinary prowess. Choose a dish that you feel most comfortable making, one you can present with confidence to the assembled clan. Whether it's a staple like baked ham with a modern asian-flavoured twist or that memory-of-Christmases-past, roast goose with fruit and nut seasoning, there's a perfect main course for you in the pages that follow. And don't forget the accompaniments: a real star needs a good supporting cast to show its talent to best advantage.

traditional turkey with forcemeat stuffing

PREPARATION TIME 40 MINUTES **COOKING TIME** 3 HOURS 10 MINUTES (PLUS STANDING TIME)

This recipe will serve between eight and 12 people depending on your menu.

4.5kg turkey

1 cup (250ml) water

80g butter, melted

¼ cup (35g) plain flour

3 cups (750ml) chicken stock

½ cup (125ml) dry white wine

FORCEMEAT STUFFING

40g butter

3 medium brown onions (450g), chopped finely

2 bacon rashers (140g), rind removed, chopped coarsely

1 cup (70g) stale breadcrumbs

2 tablespoons finely chopped fresh tarragon

½ cup coarsely chopped fresh flat-leaf parsley

½ cup (75g) coarsely chopped roasted pistachios

250g pork mince

250g chicken mince

1 Make forcemeat stuffing.

2 Preheat oven to 180°C/160°C fan-forced.

3 Discard neck from turkey. Rinse turkey under cold water; pat dry inside and out. Fill neck cavity loosely with stuffing; secure skin over opening with toothpicks. Fill large cavity loosely with stuffing; tie legs together with kitchen string.

4 Place turkey on oiled wire rack in large shallow flameproof baking dish; pour the water into dish. Brush turkey all over with half the butter; cover dish tightly with two layers of greased foil. Roast 2 hours. Uncover turkey; brush with remaining butter. Roast, uncovered, about 45 minutes or until cooked. Remove turkey from dish, cover turkey; stand 20 minutes.

5 Pour juice from dish into large jug; skim 1 tablespoon of fat from juice, return to same dish. Skim and discard remaining fat from juice. Add flour to dish; cook, stirring, until mixture is well browned. Gradually stir in stock, wine and remaining juice; bring to a boil, stirring, until gravy thickens. Strain gravy into jug; serve gravy with turkey.

FORCEMEAT STUFFING Melt butter in medium frying pan; cook onion and bacon, stirring, until onion softens. Combine onion mixture in large bowl with remaining ingredients.

TIPS To test if turkey is cooked, insert a skewer sideways into the thickest part of the thigh then remove and press flesh to release the juices. If the juice runs clear, the turkey is cooked. Alternatively, insert a meat thermometer into the thickest part of the thigh, without touching bone; it should reach 90°C. Test the seasoning, too; it should be at least 75°C. For information on how to carve a turkey, see page 72.

boned turkey buffé with couscous stuffing

PREPARATION TIME 1 HOUR **COOKING TIME** 2 HOURS

Order a 4.5kg fresh boned and butterflied turkey buffé from your butcher for this recipe. This recipe will serve between eight and 12 people depending on your menu.

½ cup (80g) sultanas

½ cup (125ml) lemon juice

4.5kg butterflied turkey buffé

1 cup (250ml) chicken stock

¼ cup (60ml) olive oil

1 cup (200g) couscous

¼ cup (40g) roasted pepitas

¼ cup (35g) roasted slivered almonds

¼ cup (35g) roasted pecans, chopped coarsely

¼ cup coarsely chopped fresh flat-leaf parsley

¼ cup coarsely chopped fresh coriander

2 eggs, beaten lightly

1 cup (250ml) water

½ cup (125ml) dry white wine

⅓ cup (50g) plain flour

2 cups (500ml) chicken stock, extra

3 cups (750ml) water, extra

PAPRIKA RUB

1 teaspoon fennel seeds

1 teaspoon sweet paprika

½ teaspoon ground ginger

2 teaspoons salt

2 cloves garlic, quartered

2 tablespoons olive oil

1 Soak sultanas in small bowl with half the juice.

2 Using mortar and pestle, crush ingredients for paprika rub until smooth.

3 Preheat oven to 180°C/160°C fan-forced.

4 Place turkey flat on board, skin-side down; cover with plastic wrap. Using rolling pin or meat mallet, flatten turkey meat to an even thickness all over.

5 Combine stock, oil and remaining juice in medium saucepan; bring to a boil. Remove from heat; stir in couscous. Cover; stand about 5 minutes or until liquid is absorbed, fluffing with fork occasionally. Stir in sultana mixture, pepitas, nuts, herbs and egg.

6 With pointed end of turkey breast facing away from you, place couscous stuffing horizontally along centre of turkey meat. Bring the pointed end of breast over stuffing, securing to the neck skin flap with toothpicks. Working from the centre out, continue securing sides of turkey together with toothpicks (you will have a rectangular roll of turkey in front of you). Tie securely with kitchen string at 4cm intervals.

7 Place turkey roll on oiled wire rack in large shallow flameproof baking dish; add the water and wine to dish. Rub turkey roll with paprika rub; cover dish tightly with two layers of greased foil. Roast 1 hour. Uncover; roast about 45 minutes or until turkey roll is cooked. Transfer turkey roll to large serving platter; cover to keep warm.

8 Place dish with juice over heat, add flour; cook, stirring, until mixture bubbles and is browned. Gradually stir in extra stock and the extra water; bring to a boil. Simmer, stirring, until gravy thickens. Strain gravy into large jug; serve with turkey.

aussie barbecued ham

PREPARATION TIME 15 MINUTES COOKING TIME 1 HOUR 45 MINUTES (PLUS STANDING TIME)

This recipe will serve between eight and 12 people depending on your menu.

7kg cooked leg of ham

2 tablespoons dijon mustard

⅔ cup (150g) firmly packed brown sugar

½ cup (125ml) pineapple juice

½ cup (125ml) sweet sherry

¼ cup (55g) firmly packed brown sugar, extra

2 cloves garlic, halved lengthways

¼ teaspoon ground clove

1 medium pineapple (1.25kg), halved, sliced thickly

1 Remove and discard rind from ham (see page 72).

2 Make shallow cuts diagonally across fat at 3cm intervals, then shallow-cut in opposite direction, forming diamond patterns. Do not cut right through top fat or fat will spread apart during cooking.

3 Place ham in disposable aluminium baking dish; rub with combined mustard and sugar. Place ham on heated barbecue; cook by indirect heat in covered barbecue following the manufacturer's instructions, 1 hour.

4 Meanwhile, combine juice, sherry, extra sugar, garlic and clove in small saucepan; stir over heat until sugar dissolves. Simmer, uncovered, about 10 minutes or until glaze reduces by half. Brush ham with glaze; cook, covered, using indirect method, 45 minutes, brushing several times with glaze during cooking. Cover ham with foil; stand 15 minutes before slicing.

5 Meanwhile, cook pineapple on heated barbecue, brushing with remaining glaze during cooking.

6 Serve ham with pineapple.

TIPS As an alternative to the Aussie flavours used above, a glaze of redcurrant cranberry sauce and port also goes beautifully with ham.

REDCURRANT CRANBERRY SAUCE AND PORT GLAZE Combine 275g jar red currant and cranberry sauce and ½ cup (125ml) water in small saucepan; stir over heat, without boiling, until sauce is smooth. Remove from heat, stir in 2 tablespoons lemon juice and ⅓ cup (80ml) port; brush over ham during last 45 minutes of cooking time.

butterflied lamb with fresh mint sauce

PREPARATION TIME 15 MINUTES (PLUS REFRIGERATION TIME) COOKING TIME 25 MINUTES SERVES 10

The mint sauce can be made several days ahead; keep refrigerated.

½ cup (125ml) water

½ cup (110g) firmly packed brown sugar

1½ cups (375ml) cider vinegar

½ cup finely chopped fresh mint

1 teaspoon salt

¼ teaspoon coarsely ground black pepper

¼ cup (90g) honey

1 tablespoon wholegrain mustard

2kg butterflied leg of lamb

¼ cup loosely packed fresh rosemary leaves

1 To make mint sauce, combine the water and sugar in small saucepan. Stir over heat, without boiling, until sugar dissolves. Simmer, uncovered, without stirring, about 5 minutes or until syrup thickens slightly. Combine syrup, vinegar, mint, salt and pepper in medium jug.

2 Place a quarter of the mint sauce in large shallow dish with honey and mustard, add lamb; coat well in mint sauce mixture. Cover; refrigerate 2 hours or overnight, turning occasionally.

3 Preheat barbecue to medium heat. Place drained lamb, fat-side down, on oiled barbecue (or grill plate). Cover lamb with foil or large upturned baking dish, cook about 10 minutes or until browned underneath. Turn lamb, sprinkle with rosemary; cook, covered, further 10 minutes or until lamb is done as desired (or, cook by indirect heat in covered barbecue following the manufacturer's instructions). Cover; stand lamb 10 minutes.

4 Serve sliced lamb with remaining mint sauce.

roast goose with fruit and nut seasoning

PREPARATION TIME 1 HOUR **COOKING TIME** 2 HOURS 15 MINUTES **SERVES** 6 TO 8

20g butter, melted

1 tablespoon honey

1 teaspoon light soy sauce

3.5kg goose

plain flour

FRUIT AND NUT SEASONING

2 tablespoons vegetable oil

200g chicken giblets,
finely chopped

1 medium brown onion (150g),
finely chopped

1 trimmed celery stalk (100g),
chopped

1 medium apple (150g), chopped

½ cup (80g) coarsely chopped
brazil nuts

½ cup (70g) silvered almonds

½ cup (75g) coarsely chopped
dried apricots

½ cup (85g) finely chopped raisins

1 tablespoon chopped fresh mint

1½ cups (100g) stale breadcrumbs

1 Preheat oven to 200°C/180°C fan-forced.

2 Make fruit and nut seasoning.

3 Combine butter, honey and sauce in small bowl, brush mixture over inside and outside of goose. Fill goose with seasoning, secure opening with skewers. Tie legs together, tuck wings under goose. Prick skin to release fat during roasting.

4 Lightly flour large oven bag; place goose in bag, secure with tie provided. Make holes in bag as advised on package. Place goose breast-side-up in baking dish, cover dish with foil; roast 1 hour. Remove foil, roast goose further 1 hour.

FRUIT AND NUT SEASONING Heat half the oil in medium saucepan, add giblets; cook, stirring, until browned; drain. Add remaining oil to pan, add onion and celery; cook, stirring, until onion is soft. Add apple and nuts; cook, stirring, until nuts are browned lightly. Remove from heat, stir in giblets, apricots, raisins, mint and breadcrumbs; cool.

slow-cooked duck with cabbage, fennel and balsamic roasted potatoes

PREPARATION TIME 20 MINUTES **COOKING TIME** 2 HOURS 20 MINUTES **SERVES** 4

½ small red cabbage (600g), cut into four wedges

1 large leek (500g), chopped coarsely

4 baby fennel bulbs (520g), trimmed, halved lengthways

1 tablespoon fresh rosemary leaves

2 cloves garlic, sliced thinly

1 cup (250ml) chicken stock

⅓ cup (80ml) cider vinegar

2 tablespoons redcurrant jelly

4 duck marylands (1.2kg), trimmed

1 tablespoon salt

BALSAMIC ROASTED POTATOES

1kg small potatoes, halved

30g butter, melted

2 tablespoons balsamic vinegar

1 Preheat oven to 160°C/140°C fan-forced.

2 Combine cabbage, leek, fennel, rosemary, garlic, stock, vinegar and jelly in medium deep baking dish. Rub duck skin with salt; place duck, skin-side up, on cabbage mixture. Cook, uncovered, about 2¼ hours or until duck meat is tender and skin is crisp.

3 Make balsamic roasted potatoes.

4 Strain pan juices through muslin-lined sieve into medium saucepan; cover duck and cabbage mixture. Skim fat from surface of pan juices; boil, uncovered, about 5 minutes or until sauce thickens slightly.

5 Serve duck on cabbage mixture, accompanied with potatoes; drizzle with sauce.

BALSAMIC ROASTED POTATOES Combine potatoes, butter and vinegar in medium baking dish. Roast, uncovered, alongside the duck, for the last 1¼ hours of the duck cooking time or until potatoes are tender and browned lightly. Brush potatoes occasionally with vinegar mixture in dish.

Brushing them with the combined butter and balsamic vinegar during cooking gives the finished potatoes a beautiful mahogany-coloured glaze.

mains ❄ modern

hot seafood platter

PREPARATION TIME 40 MINUTES (PLUS REFRIGERATION TIME) **COOKING TIME** 25 MINUTES **SERVES** 4

500g dhufish cutlets, skinned

500g calamari rings

1 cup (150g) plain flour

¼ cup (60ml) milk

2 eggs, beaten lightly

2 cups (140g) stale breadcrumbs

⅓ cup finely chopped fresh flat-leaf parsley

½ cup (40g) finely grated parmesan

1 tablespoon finely grated lemon rind

1 medium tomato (190g), halved

1 tablespoon vodka

¼ teaspoon Tabasco sauce

2 teaspoons worcestershire sauce

1 teaspoon lemon juice

vegetable oil, for shallow-frying

12 oysters, on the half shell

1 trimmed celery stalk (100g), chopped finely

3 slices pancetta (45g), chopped finely

8 uncooked large king prawns (560g)

2 lemons, cut into wedges

1 Halve fish lengthways, discard bones; cut each half into three pieces. Coat fish and calamari in flour then in combined milk and egg, and finally in combined breadcrumbs, parsley, cheese and rind. Cover; refrigerate 15 minutes.

2 Grate tomato halves coarsely into small bowl; discard skin. Stir in vodka, sauces and juice.

3 Heat oil in large deep frying pan; shallow-fry fish and calamari, in batches, until cooked. Drain.

4 Preheat grill.

5 Place oysters on oven tray. Divide tomato mixture among oysters; top with celery and pancetta. Grill about 3 minutes or until pancetta is crisp.

6 Cook prawns on heated oiled grill plate (or grill or barbecue) until cooked. Serve seafood with lemon wedges on platter.

TIPS You can substitute your favourite white fish fillets for the dhufish in this recipe.
Serve with the dipping sauces from the cold seafood platter (page 52).

cold seafood platter with dipping sauces

PREPARATION TIME 1 HOUR SERVES 4

1 cooked large lobster (1.2kg)
2 cooked blue swimmer crabs (650g)
4 cooked balmain bugs (800g)
16 cooked large king prawns (1kg)
12 oysters, on the half shell
3 medium lemons (420g)
cut into wedges

1 To prepare lobster, place lobster upside-down, cut through chest and tail; turn lobster around and cut through the head. Pull halves apart; use a small spoon to remove brain matter and liver. Rinse lobster carefully under cold water. Remove lobster meat from the shell with fingers; it should lift out easily in a single large piece. Pat dry.

2 To prepare crabs, lift tail flap then, with a peeling motion, lift off the back shell. Remove and discard whitish gills, liver and brain matter; rinse crab well. Rinse under cold water; cut crab bodies into halves.

3 Place bugs upside-down on chopping board; cut in half lengthways. Remove any green matter, liver and back vein from tails.

4 Shell and devein prawns, leaving heads and tails intact.

5 Serve seafood with lemon wedges and dipping sauces (page 52).

TIP For information on how to prepare lobster and crab, see page 73.

dipping sauces for cold seafood platter

SAMBAL MAYONNAISE
PREPARATION TIME 5 MINUTES MAKES ¾ CUP

½ cup (150g) mayonnaise

1 tablespoon water

2 tablespoons tomato sauce

1 teaspoon worcestershire sauce

1 teaspoon sambal oelek

1 Combine ingredients in small bowl.

SOY AND MIRIN
PREPARATION TIME 5 MINUTES MAKES ½ CUP

2 tablespoons water

1 tablespoon light soy sauce

2 tablespoons mirin

2 teaspoons rice vinegar

½ teaspoon sambal oelek

1 Combine ingredients in small bowl.

CHILLI AND LIME
PREPARATION TIME 5 MINUTES MAKES ½ CUP

¼ cup (60ml) sweet chilli sauce

2 tablespoons lime juice

1 tablespoon water

1 teaspoon fish sauce

2 teaspoons finely chopped fresh
vietnamese mint

1 Combine ingredients in small bowl.

MUSTARD AND DILL
PREPARATION TIME 5 MINUTES MAKES ⅔ CUP

½ cup (150g) mayonnaise

1 tablespoon water

1 tablespoon drained baby capers, rinsed

1 teaspoon wholegrain mustard

1 tablespoon coarsely chopped fresh dill

1 Combine ingredients in small bowl.

Clockwise from top: sambal mayonnaise;
chilli and lime; mustard and dill; soy and mirin.

whole poached salmon with dill yogurt sauce

PREPARATION TIME 15 MINUTES **COOKING TIME** 20 MINUTES **SERVES** 10

2kg whole salmon or ocean trout

2 sprigs fresh dill

2 sprigs fresh flat-leaf parsley

¼ teaspoon black peppercorns

1 cup (250ml) dry white wine

DILL YOGURT SAUCE

500g greek-style yogurt

2 shallots (50g), chopped finely

1 tablespoon finely chopped fresh dill

1 tablespoon finely chopped fresh chives

1 Wipe fish dry. Place fish, herbs, peppercorns and wine in fish poacher or flameproof baking dish. Add enough water to completely cover fish. Bring slowly to a simmer (the liquid must not boil).

2 Poach fish about 12 minutes (or 10 minutes for every 2.5cm thickness). When the large fin in the centre back comes away easily from the bone, the fish is cooked.

3 Combine ingredients for dill yogurt sauce in small bowl.

4 Drain fish well, transfer to platter; discard liquid and herbs. Remove skin from top of fish. Serve with sauce, lemon wedges and fresh herbs, if desired.

TIPS Fish can be poached several hours ahead.
The dill yogurt sauce can be made several hours ahead.

slow-roasted pesto salmon

PREPARATION TIME 20 MINUTES **COOKING TIME** 45 MINUTES **SERVES 8**

1 cup loosely packed fresh
basil leaves

2 cloves garlic, quartered

2 tablespoons roasted pine nuts

2 tablespoons lemon juice

¼ cup (60ml) olive oil

1.5kg piece salmon fillet, skin on

1 tablespoon olive oil, extra

2 large red capsicums (700g),
chopped coarsely

1 large red onion (300g),
chopped coarsely

1 Preheat oven to 160°C/140°C fan-forced.

2 Blend or process basil, garlic, nuts and juice until combined. With motor operating, gradually add oil in a thin, steady stream until pesto thickens slightly.

3 Place fish, skin-side down, on piece of oiled foil large enough to completely enclose fish; coat fish with half of the pesto. Enclose fish in foil. Place parcel on oven tray; roast about 45 minutes or until cooked.

4 Heat extra oil in large frying pan; cook capsicum and onion, stirring, until onion softens.

5 Serve fish topped with onion mixture and remaining pesto.

TIP If the pesto is too thick for your liking, thin it down with a little olive oil before drizzling over salmon.

whole snapper wrapped in banana leaf

PREPARATION TIME 45 MINUTES COOKING TIME 45 MINUTES SERVES 10

3 large banana leaves

⅓ cup (110g) thai chilli jam

2 tablespoons light soy sauce

1 tablespoon chinese rice wine

1 whole snapper (2kg)

6cm piece fresh ginger (30g), cut into matchsticks

1 small carrot (70g), cut into matchsticks

2 cloves garlic, crushed

227g can drained, rinsed bamboo shoots, cut into matchsticks

2 green onions, chopped coarsely

½ cup firmly packed fresh coriander leaves

2 limes, cut into wedges

1 Trim two banana leaves to make one 30cm x 50cm rectangle and two 15cm x 30cm rectangles. Using metal tongs, dip one piece at a time into large saucepan of boiling water; remove immediately. Rinse under cold water; pat dry. Trim remaining banana leaf to fit grill plate.

2 Combine jam, sauce and wine in small bowl.

3 Score fish both sides through thickest part of flesh; place on large tray, brush both sides with jam mixture.

4 Combine ginger, carrot, garlic, bamboo and onion in medium bowl.

5 Place 30cm x 50cm leaf on work surface. Place one 15cm x 30cm leaf in centre of larger leaf; top with fish. Pour over any remaining jam mixture. Top fish with ginger mixture and remaining 15cm x 30cm leaf. Fold corners of banana leaf into centre to enclose fish; tie parcel at 10cm intervals with kitchen string to secure.

6 Place remaining trimmed leaf onto heated grill plate (or grill or barbecue); place fish parcel on leaf. Cook, over medium heat, about 40 minutes or until fish is cooked, turning halfway through cooking time.

7 Serve fish sprinkled with coriander leaves and lime wedges.

TIPS Any whole firm-fleshed fish can be used for this recipe.
Foil can be used if banana leaves are unavailable. Banana leaves can be ordered from fruit and vegetable shops.
Thai chilli jam is a combination of garlic, shallots, chilli, tomato paste, fish sauce, galangal, spices and shrimp paste. It is sold under various names, and can be found in the Asian food section of the supermarket.

whole fish in a salt crust with gremolata

PREPARATION TIME 10 MINUTES **COOKING TIME** 35 MINUTES **SERVES 8**

Gremolata can be made several hours ahead.

2 x 1kg whole snapper, cleaned, scales left on

3kg coarse cooking salt, approximately

GREMOLATA

½ cup finely chopped fresh flat-leaf parsley

2 cloves garlic, crushed

1 tablespoon finely grated lemon rind

2 tablespoons extra virgin olive oil

1 Preheat oven to 240°C/220°C fan-forced.

2 Combine gremolata ingredients in small bowl.

3 Wash fish, pat dry inside and out. Fill cavities of fish with half the gremolata.

4 Divide half the salt between two ovenproof trays large enough to hold fish (ovenproof metal oval platters are ideal). Place fish on salt.

5 Place remaining salt in large sieve or colander and run quickly under cold water until salt is damp. Press salt firmly over fish to completely cover fish.

6 Bake 35 minutes. Remove fish from oven; stand 5 minutes.

7 Using a hammer or meat mallet and old knife, break open the crust then lift away with the scales and skin.

8 Serve fish with remaining gremolata.

TIPS You can use different types of whole fish that weigh about 1kg each. Make sure the fish and tray will fit into the oven. Coarse sea salt can also be used; it is available from supermarkets or health food stores. Rock salt should not be used in this recipe.

roast veal rack with herb stuffing

PREPARATION TIME 20 MINUTES COOKING TIME 35 MINUTES SERVES 4

1 small brown onion (80g), chopped finely

1 clove garlic, crushed

½ trimmed celery stalk (50g), chopped finely

¾ cup (45g) stale breadcrumbs

1 tablespoon dijon mustard

1 teaspoon finely chopped fresh thyme

1 tablespoon finely chopped fresh flat-leaf parsley

1 teaspoon finely grated lemon rind

2 teaspoons sea salt

2 teaspoons cracked black pepper

1 x 4 french-trimmed veal cutlet rack

1 medium brown onion (150g), chopped coarsely

1½ cups (375ml) beef stock

2 teaspoons olive oil

2 teaspoons balsamic vinegar

½ cup (125ml) beef stock, extra

1 Preheat oven to 220°C/200°C fan-forced.

2 Cook finely chopped onion, garlic and celery in heated oiled small frying pan, stirring, until vegetables soften. Add breadcrumbs; cook until breadcrumbs brown lightly. Remove from heat; stir in mustard, herbs, rind, half of the salt and half of the pepper. Cool 10 minutes.

3 Meanwhile, make a tunnel through veal rack, close to the bone; fill with herb mixture.

4 Place coarsely chopped onion and stock in large flameproof baking dish; add veal, drizzle with oil, sprinkle with remaining salt and pepper. Roast, uncovered, in oven about 30 minutes or until cooked. Remove veal from dish, cover; stand 10 minutes.

5 Stir vinegar and extra stock into veal juices in dish; bring to a boil. Strain into medium jug; serve with veal.

pork loin with spinach and pancetta stuffing

PREPARATION TIME 30 MINUTES   **COOKING TIME** 1 HOUR 30 MINUTES

This recipe will serve between eight and 12 people depending on your menu.

4 slices white bread (120g)

2 tablespoons olive oil

1 clove garlic, crushed

1 medium brown onion (150g), chopped coarsely

6 slices pancetta (90g), chopped coarsely

100g baby spinach leaves

¼ cup (35g) roasted macadamias, chopped coarsely

½ cup (125ml) chicken stock

2kg boned pork loin

PLUM AND RED WINE SAUCE

1½ cups (480g) plum jam

2 tablespoons dry red wine

⅔ cup (160ml) chicken stock

1 Preheat oven to 200°C/180°C fan-forced.

2 To make croutons; discard bread crusts, cut bread into 1cm cubes. Heat half of the oil in large frying pan; cook bread until browned and crisp. Drain.

3 Heat remaining oil in same pan; cook garlic, onion and pancetta until onion browns lightly. Stir in spinach; remove from heat. Stir in croutons, nuts and stock.

4 Place pork on board, fat-side down; slice through thickest part of pork horizontally, without cutting through other side. Open out pork to form one large piece; press stuffing mixture against loin along width of pork. Roll pork to enclose stuffing, securing with kitchen string at 2cm intervals.

5 Place rolled pork on rack in large, shallow baking dish. Roast about 1¼ hours or until cooked through. Cover, stand pork 10 minutes.

6 Meanwhile, make plum and red wine sauce. Serve sliced pork with sauce.

PLUM AND RED WINE SAUCE Combine ingredients in small saucepan; simmer, uncovered, about 10 minutes or until sauce thickens slightly.

TIP When ordering the pork, ask your butcher to leave a flap measuring about 20cm in length to help make rolling the stuffed loin easier.

Slice through thickest part of the pork, taking care not to cut all the way through.

Press stuffing mixture against loin across the entire width of the pork.

Roll pork to enclose stuffing, securing with kitchen string at 2cm intervals.

slow-roasted turkey with zucchini, lemon and wild rice seasoning

PREPARATION TIME 40 MINUTES **COOKING TIME** 4 HOURS 45 MINUTES **SERVES** 10

4kg turkey

50cm square muslin

100g butter, melted

1 litre (4 cups) water

40g butter

¼ cup (35g) plain flour

⅓ cup (80ml) port

2 cups (500ml) chicken stock

ZUCCHINI, LEMON AND WILD RICE SEASONING

50g butter

1 large brown onion (200g), chopped coarsely

2 cloves garlic, crushed

⅓ cup (60g) wild rice

½ cup (125ml) dry white wine

1 cup (250ml) water

⅔ cup (130g) basmati rice

2 cups (500ml) chicken stock

2 medium zucchini (240g), grated coarsely

2 teaspoons finely grated lemon rind

2 teaspoons lemon thyme leaves

1 cup (70g) stale breadcrumbs

1 Make zucchini, lemon and wild rice seasoning.

2 Preheat oven to 150°C/130°C fan-forced.

3 Discard neck from turkey. Rinse turkey under cold water, pat dry inside and out. Fill neck cavity with seasoning; secure skin over opening with toothpicks. Fill large cavity with seasoning; tie legs together with string, tuck wing tips under turkey.

4 Place turkey on oiled wire rack in flameproof baking dish. Dip muslin in melted butter and place it over turkey. Add the water to baking dish, cover dish with foil. Roast 4 hours.

5 Remove foil and muslin from turkey, brush with pan juices. Increase oven temperature to 200°C/180°C fan-forced; roast further 30 minutes or until turkey is cooked. Remove turkey from oven; cover, stand 20 minutes.

6 Drain pan juices into large jug; skim fat from top of juices, discard. You will need about 2 cups of juice.

7 Place same baking dish over medium heat, melt butter, add flour; cook, stirring, until well browned. Gradually stir in port, reserved juices and stock; cook, stirring, until mixture boils and thickens. Strain into large jug.

8 Serve turkey with gravy.

ZUCCHINI, LEMON AND WILD RICE SEASONING Heat butter in large frying pan, add onion and garlic; cook, stirring, until onion is soft. Add wild rice; cook, stirring, 1 minute. Add wine; simmer, covered, about 10 minutes or until almost all the liquid is absorbed. Add the water; simmer, covered, about 10 minutes, until liquid is absorbed. Add basmati rice; cook, stirring, 1 minute. Add stock; simmer, covered, 10 minutes or until all liquid is absorbed and rice is tender. Stir in zucchini, rind and thyme; cool. Add breadcrumbs; mix well.

TIPS The seasoning can be made a day ahead, refrigerate separately. Fill turkey with seasoning close to cooking.
To keep leftover turkey, remove seasoning from cavity and refrigerate separately.
For information on how to carve a turkey, see page 72.

asian-style baked ham

PREPARATION TIME 15 MINUTES (PLUS REFRIGERATION TIME) **COOKING TIME** 1 HOUR 30 MINUTES

This recipe will serve between eight and 12 people depending on your menu.

7kg cooked leg of ham

1 cup (250ml) light soy sauce

¾ cup (180ml) dry sherry

⅓ cup (75g) firmly packed brown sugar

⅓ cup (120g) honey

2 teaspoons red food colouring

4 cloves garlic, crushed

2 teaspoons five-spice powder

60 cloves (approximately)

1 Remove and discard rind from ham (see page 72).

2 Make shallow cuts diagonally across fat at 3cm intervals, then shallow-cut in opposite direction, forming diamond patterns. Do not cut through top fat or fat will spread apart during cooking.

3 Combine sauce, sherry, sugar, honey, colouring, garlic and five-spice in small bowl. Place ham on wire rack in large baking dish; brush with soy mixture. Centre one clove in each diamond, cover; refrigerate overnight.

4 Preheat oven to 180°C/160°C fan-forced.

5 Place ham on wire rack in large baking dish; pour marinade into medium jug. Cover ham with greased foil; bake 1 hour. Uncover; bake about 30 minutes or until ham is lightly caramelised, brushing frequently with marinade during cooking.

TIP As an alternative to the Asian flavours used above, a glaze of orange, ginger and maple syrup also goes beautifully with this ham.

ORANGE MARMALADE GLAZE Combine 1 cup (250ml) maple syrup, 1 cup (250ml) fresh orange juice, ⅓ cup (115g) orange marmalade, 12cm piece fresh ginger (60g), grated, and 2 teaspoons finely grated orange rind in small saucepan. Simmer, uncovered, 15 minutes then strain before brushing over ham during baking.

lemon thyme and chilli roast spatchcock

PREPARATION TIME 30 MINUTES (PLUS REFRIGERATION TIME) COOKING TIME 40 MINUTES SERVES 10

5 spatchcocks (2.5kg), quartered

1 tablespoon fresh lemon thyme leaves

LEMON THYME AND CHILLI MARINADE

2 fresh long red chillies, chopped finely

2 cloves garlic, crushed

1 tablespoon fresh lemon thyme leaves

2 teaspoons finely grated lemon rind

¼ cup (60ml) lemon juice

2 tablespoons olive oil

2 tablespoons balsamic vinegar

2 tablespoons honey

1 Combine ingredients for lemon thyme and chilli marinade in screw-top jar; shake well.

2 Combine three-quarters of the marinade with spatchcock in large shallow dish. Cover; refrigerate 3 hours or overnight. Refrigerate remaining marinade until required.

3 Preheat oven to 220°C/200°C fan-forced.

4 Place spatchcock, in single layer, on wire racks in large shallow baking dishes. Roast spatchcock, uncovered, about 40 minutes or until cooked.

5 Serve spatchcock drizzled with reserved marinade and sprinkled with thyme leaves.

beef with herb and walnut crust

PREPARATION TIME 20 MINUTES COOKING TIME 35 MINUTES SERVES 6

750g piece beef fillet

1 tablespoon olive oil

½ cup coarsely chopped fresh flat-leaf parsley

¼ cup coarsely chopped fresh dill

1 clove garlic, crushed

2 teaspoons finely grated lemon rind

2 teaspoons lemon juice

¼ cup (30g) coarsely chopped roasted walnuts

1 tablespoon olive oil, extra

1 Preheat oven to 200°C/180°C fan-forced.

2 Rub beef with oil.

3 Combine remaining ingredients in small bowl.

4 Cook beef, in flameproof baking dish, over high heat until browned all over.

5 Roast beef, uncovered, in oven, 15 minutes. Remove, sprinkle with three-quarters of the parsley mixture. Cover, return to oven; roast further 10 minutes or until cooked. Remove from oven, stand 10 minutes. Serve beef, sliced, sprinkled with remaining parsley mixture.

TIP The herb and walnut mixture can be made several hours ahead.

hints Mains like these need to be eaten hot, not such an easy feat when you're juggling several courses and moving various dishes in and out of your oven at different times. Another preparation possibility to consider is to make use of your barbecue: both the spatchcock and the beef lend themselves well to being cooked by indirect heat, in a covered barbecue, in just about the same time that they would take in the oven. Serving main courses like these on platters enhances the sense of celebration, and allows everyone a chance to admire them before digging in. Don't forget to rest the beef before carving it, to allow the juices to settle.

mains ❋ a little extra help

There's more detail involved when preparing your main ingredient than just the cooking, and these simple photos are worth a thousand words when it comes to explaining how to make your presentation picture-perfect.

how to carve ham

1 Make a circular cut through rind about 10cm from end of shank; run fingers under edge of rind then pull rind back from cut.

2 Take long sweeps with the knife against the cut surface to get large thin slices. As you carve, slices will increase in size.

3 As you continue slicing the ham, turn it around, adjusting it on the ham stand so that it can be carved from the side.

how to carve turkey

1 Remove wing, then thigh and drumstick on one side of turkey, cutting through thigh bone at the joint where it joins the body.

2 Place cut-off section under bird to keep it stable; holding turkey with a fork, carve across the breast at top, along the torso.

3 Separate and carve drumstick and thigh then turn the bird over and carve the other side in exactly the same manner.

preparing lobster

 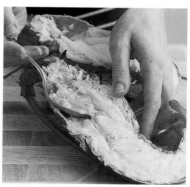 

1 Turn the lobster upside-down and cut through chest and tail; turn the lobster around and cut through the head.

2 Pull the two halves apart and, using a small spoon, remove brain matter and liver. Rinse the lobster under cold running water.

3 Using your fingers, carefully remove lobster meat from the shell; it should lift out easily in a single piece.

preparing crab

1 Cooked or raw crabs are treated in the same manner: lift up the tail flap, then using a peeling motion, lift off the back shell.

2 Remove and discard the whitish gills as well as the liver and brain matter; rinse crab thoroughly under cold running water.

3 Crack body shell and remove the meat then crack crab claws carefully to avoid getting shell splinters mixed with the flesh.

white bean salad with coriander, mint and lemon grass

PREPARATION TIME 15 MINUTES **SERVES** 4

2 x 400g cans cannellini beans, rinsed, drained

150g baby spinach leaves

1 small red onion (100g), sliced thinly

1 clove garlic, crushed

1 tablespoon coarsely chopped fresh coriander

1 tablespoon coarsely chopped fresh mint

1 tablespoon thinly sliced fresh lemon grass

1cm piece fresh ginger (5g), grated

2 tablespoons sesame oil

2 tablespoons soy sauce

2 tablespoons sweet chilli sauce

2 tablespoons lime juice

1 teaspoon honey

2 fresh small red thai chillies, sliced thinly

1 Combine beans in large bowl with spinach and onion.

2 Combine garlic, herbs, lemon grass, ginger, oil, sauces, juice and honey in screw-top jar; shake well.

3 Just before serving, drizzle dressing over salad; toss gently then sprinkle with chilli.

hints These two accompaniments are a real feast for the eyes as well as the tastebuds – their vibrant colours even suit the traditional Christmas colour theme of reds and greens. Both the tomatoes and the salad are to be cooked as close to serving time as possible but can be partially prepared ahead: mix the garlic, oil and vinegar in a bowl, then gently stir in the tomatoes and allow to stand until you're ready to roast them and crisp the basil; for the salad, the dressing can be made in the morning and the prosciutto grilled, broken into pieces and set aside, in an airtight container, at the same time. Haloumi is one ingredient that has to be eaten as soon as it's grilled; if you prefer, you can satisfactorily substitute smoked mozzarella, which needs no cooking, in this salad.

roasted truss tomatoes with crispy basil leaves

PREPARATION TIME 10 MINUTES **COOKING TIME** 10 MINUTES **SERVES** 8

500g baby vine-ripened
truss tomatoes

2 cloves garlic, sliced thinly

1 tablespoon olive oil

2 teaspoons balsamic vinegar

vegetable oil, for deep-frying

⅓ cup loosely packed fresh
basil leaves

1 Preheat oven to 180°C/160°C fan-forced.

2 Place tomatoes on oven tray; pour over combined garlic, oil and vinegar. Roast about 10 minutes or until tomatoes soften.

3 Meanwhile, heat vegetable oil in small saucepan; deep-fry basil, in batches, until crisp.

4 Serve tomatoes sprinkled with basil.

TIP Be careful when deep-frying the basil. The water content of herbs will cause the oil to bubble and spit. Use a small, deep saucepan with about 3cm oil.

haloumi, prosciutto and spinach salad

PREPARATION TIME 15 MINUTES **COOKING TIME** 15 MINUTES **SERVES** 8

13 prosciutto slices (200g)

500g asparagus, trimmed

200g haloumi cheese,
sliced thinly

2 small pears (360g), cored,
cut into thin wedges

200g baby spinach leaves

MACADAMIA DRESSING

½ cup (75g) roasted macadamias,
chopped coarsely

2 tablespoons sherry vinegar

¼ cup (60ml) macadamia oil

1 Preheat grill.

2 Cook prosciutto under grill until crisp; break into bite-size pieces.

3 Boil, steam or microwave asparagus until just tender; drain.

4 Combine ingredients for macadamia dressing in screw-top jar; shake well.

5 Cook asparagus, cheese and pear on heated, oiled grill plate (or grill or barbecue) until browned lightly.

6 Place prosciutto, asparagus, cheese, pear and spinach in large bowl with dressing; toss gently to combine.

TIP You can substitute olive oil for the macadamia oil, if you prefer.

the perfect potato salad

PREPARATION TIME 20 MINUTES (PLUS REFRIGERATION TIME) **COOKING TIME** 20 MINUTES **SERVES** 8

Crisp, low-starch potatoes, such as bintje, desiree, kipfler and sebago, make the best potato salad. Take care not to overcook them or they will break apart or crumble.

2kg sebago potatoes, peeled

2 tablespoons cider vinegar

8 green onions, sliced thinly

¼ cup finely chopped fresh flat-leaf parsley

MAYONNAISE

2 egg yolks

1 teaspoon dijon mustard

2 teaspoons lemon juice

1 cup (250ml) vegetable oil

2 tablespoons hot water, approximately

1 Cut potatoes into 1.5cm pieces. Place potato in large saucepan, barely cover with cold water; simmer, uncovered, stirring occasionally, until just tender. Drain, spread potato on tray; sprinkle with vinegar. Cool 10 minutes. Refrigerate, covered, until cold.

2 Make mayonnaise.

3 Place potato in large bowl with mayonnaise, onion and parsley; mix gently.

MAYONNAISE Blend or process egg yolks, mustard and juice until smooth. With motor operating, gradually add oil in a thin, steady stream; process until mixture thickens. Add as much of the hot water as required to thin mayonnaise. Makes 1 cup.

balsamic-glazed baby onions

PREPARATION TIME 10 MINUTES **COOKING TIME** 15 MINUTES **SERVES** 8

1 tablespoon balsamic vinegar

1 tablespoon wholegrain mustard

¼ cup (90g) honey

2 tablespoons vegetable oil

500g baby brown onions, halved

1 Combine vinegar, mustard and honey in small saucepan; bring to a boil; simmer, uncovered, about 5 minutes or until glaze thickens.

2 Heat oil in large frying pan; cook onions, brushing constantly with glaze, stirring, until browned and cooked.

hints Everyone has a different opinion about what a perfect potato salad should be – hot or cold, creamy or vinaigrette-dressed, with bacon bits or just flavoured with onion and herbs – but you'll find it hard to find one better than this. Stirring the potatoes occasionally while they're cooking ensures they cook evenly (with no surprise hard centres after the salad is made). But take care not to overcook them or they can break apart and crumble when you mix the salad. The key to making these caramelised-looking onions is the mixture of balsamic vinegar, mustard and honey: once combined over heat with the onions, the glaze becomes almost jewel-like in appearance.

perfect roast potatoes

PREPARATION TIME 15 MINUTES
COOKING TIME 55 MINUTES **SERVES** 8

12 medium pontiac potatoes (2.5kg),
halved lengthways

⅓ cup (80ml) olive oil

1 Preheat oven to 220°C/200°C fan-forced.

2 Boil, steam or microwave potatoes 5 minutes;
drain. Pat dry; cool 10 minutes.

3 Rake rounded sides of potatoes gently with tines
of fork; place potatoes, cut-side down, in single
layer, on oiled oven tray. Brush with oil; roast, in
oven, about 50 minutes or until potatoes are
browned lightly and crisp.

mediterranean potato mash

PREPARATION TIME 25 MINUTES
COOKING TIME 20 MINUTES **SERVES** 8

2.5kg sebago potatoes, chopped coarsely

100g butter, softened

1½ cups (375ml) hot milk

½ cup (75g) drained sun-dried tomatoes,
chopped coarsely

¼ cup coarsely chopped fresh flat-leaf parsley

¼ cup (60ml) balsamic vinegar

2 tablespoons olive oil

1 Boil, steam or microwave potato until tender; drain.

2 Mash potato in large bowl with butter and milk until
smooth. Stir in tomato and parsley.

3 Serve mash drizzled with combined vinegar and oil.

barbecued kipflers

PREPARATION TIME 10 MINUTES
COOKING TIME 30 MINUTES **SERVES** 8

12 kipfler potatoes (1.5kg), unpeeled

2 tablespoons fresh oregano leaves

¼ cup loosely packed fresh thyme leaves

1 tablespoon coarsely grated lemon rind

2 cloves garlic, crushed

⅓ cup (80ml) olive oil

¼ cup (60ml) lemon juice

1 Boil, steam or microwave potatoes until tender; drain. Halve potatoes lengthways.

2 Combine herbs, rind, garlic and oil in large bowl, add potatoes; toss to coat in mixture. Cook potatoes on heated oiled grill plate (or grill or barbecue) about 15 minutes or until browned and tender.

3 Serve potatoes drizzled with juice.

honey mustard glazed roasted kumara

PREPARATION TIME 10 MINUTES
COOKING TIME 1 HOUR **SERVES** 8

2.5kg kumara, unpeeled

⅔ cup (240g) honey

⅓ cup (95g) wholegrain mustard

2 tablespoons coarsely chopped fresh rosemary

1 Preheat oven to 220°C/200°C fan-forced.

2 Halve kumara lengthways; cut each half into 2cm wedges.

3 Combine remaining ingredients in large bowl, add kumara; toss to coat in mixture. Divide kumara mixture between two large, shallow baking dishes. Roast about 1 hour or until kumara is tender and slightly caramelised.

baby beetroot with caper vinaigrette

PREPARATION TIME 10 MINUTES **COOKING TIME** 20 MINUTES **SERVES** 8

You need two bunches of baby beetroot for this recipe.

1kg baby beetroots

1 tablespoon drained baby capers, rinsed

2 tablespoons white wine vinegar

2 tablespoons olive oil

1 teaspoon dijon mustard

1 Remove stems from beetroot; cook beetroot in large saucepan of boiling water, uncovered, about 20 minutes or until tender. Drain; cool 10 minutes, peel beetroot.

2 Combine beetroot in large bowl with remaining ingredients, toss gently.

snow pea stir-fry with sesame seeds and pine nuts

PREPARATION TIME 10 MINUTES **COOKING TIME** 10 MINUTES **SERVES** 4

1 tablespoon sesame oil

2 tablespoons roasted pine nuts

1 tablespoon roasted sesame seeds

600g snow peas, trimmed

2 green onions, sliced thinly

1 Heat oil in wok; add nuts and seeds, stir-fry until browned lightly. Add snow peas and onion; stir-fry about 5 minutes or until snow peas are just tender.

hints Baby beetroots are a perfect side to have with ham or turkey: just think about how good their grown-up cousins taste sliced on sandwiches made with either of those meats. Their size means they don't take any time at all to cook, plus they have a smoother, softer texture than their adult counterpart. Because it's served cold or at room temperature, the beetroot vinaigrette can be prepared a day ahead. Of course, the snow-pea stir-fry has to be made just before serving, but if you trim the peas and ready the rest of the ingredients beforehand, a quick whip around the wok is all it takes to get this yummy side on the table with the rest of the main course.

hints Our pasta salad continues the festive colour scheme, mixing green and reddish-purple opal basil leaves among the ingredients. Purple, or opal, basil has an intense aroma and longer shelf-life than sweet basil, and can be found at most greengrocers – as can the chervil found in the mixed green salad (along with the rocket, snow peas, green beans, parsley and snap peas). Chervil is a highly underrated and all-too-infrequently used herb in this country; the French include it in their staple, *fines herbes* (along with chives, parsley and tarragon), used in the seasoning of omelettes and long-simmering meat and fish dishes. While this aromatic feathery green herb tastes somewhat like a delicious blend of fennel and celery, it is, in fact, a member of the carrot family.

green vegetable salad with american mustard dressing

PREPARATION TIME 10 MINUTES **COOKING TIME** 10 MINUTES **SERVES 4**

100g green beans, trimmed

100g snow peas, trimmed

100g sugar snap peas, trimmed

½ cup loosely packed fresh flat-leaf parsley leaves

4 tablespoons fresh chervil leaves

2 cups (50g) baby rocket leaves

2 tablespoons dried currants

AMERICAN MUSTARD DRESSING

1 tablespoon american mustard

1 tablespoon fresh lemon juice

1 tablespoon olive oil

1 Boil, steam or microwave beans and peas, separately, until just tender; drain. Rinse under cold water; drain.

2 Combine ingredients for american mustard dressing in screw-top jar; shake well.

3 Combine beans and peas in medium bowl with herbs, rocket and currants.

4 Serve salad drizzled with dressing.

pasta salad with garlic vinaigrette

PREPARATION TIME 15 MINUTES **COOKING TIME** 10 MINUTES **SERVES 6**

375g penne

200g sun-dried tomatoes in oil

½ cup (80g) roasted pine nuts, chopped coarsely

400g bocconcini, chopped coarsely

1 small red onion (100g), sliced thinly

12 fresh purple basil leaves, torn

12 fresh basil leaves, torn

2 cloves garlic, crushed

1 tablespoon dijon mustard

¼ cup (60ml) lemon juice

1 Cook pasta in large saucepan of boiling water, uncovered, until just tender; drain. Rinse under cold water; drain.

2 Drain tomatoes; reserve oil. Slice tomatoes thickly.

3 Combine pasta and tomato in large bowl with nuts, cheese, onion and both basils.

4 Combine reserved oil and remaining ingredients in screw-top jar; shake well. Drizzle dressing over salad; toss gently.

TIPS This recipe should be assembled just before serving. You can use your favourite short pasta instead of the penne, if you like.

sweet dishes

At holiday time, it's not just the kids that still have room for dessert even while groaning about how full they are. Young and old faces alike light up with smiles when the cakes and puddings, tarts and cheesecakes, sorbets and ice-creams begin their magical procession from kitchen to dining table as the meal arrives at its grand finale. And don't forget about the treats to have with coffee: truffles, shortbread, mini mince tarts (which would also make excellent gifts if they ever lasted long enough to be gift-wrapped). Lusciously rich afters are part and parcel of the whole celebratory dining experience; without them, it just wouldn't be Christmas.

grand marnier christmas cake

PREPARATION TIME 45 MINUTES (PLUS STANDING TIME) **COOKING TIME** 3 HOURS

3 cups (500g) sultanas

½ cup (100g) glacé cherries

1½ cups (250g) raisins, chopped coarsely

1½ cups (115g) seeded dates, chopped coarsely

½ cup (125g) glacé apricots, chopped coarsely

½ cup (125g) glacé pineapple, chopped coarsely

¼ cup (85g) orange marmalade

¾ cup (180ml) Grand Marnier (or brandy or rum)

250g butter, softened

¾ cup (165g) firmly packed dark brown sugar

4 eggs

2 cups (300g) plain flour

2 teaspoons mixed spice

1 cup (160g) roasted almonds, chopped coarsely

¼ cup (60ml) Grand Marnier, extra

DECORATIONS

¼ cup (55g) caster sugar

¼ cup (60ml) water

500g packet soft icing

icing sugar, for dusting

christmas tree biscuit cutter

coloured cachous

ribbon

1 Combine fruit, marmalade and liqueur in large bowl; mix well, cover tightly with plastic wrap. Store mixture in cool, dark place overnight or up to a week, stirring every day.

2 Preheat oven to 150°C/130°C fan-forced. Line base and sides of deep 19cm-square cake pan with two layers of brown and two layers of baking paper, bringing paper 5cm above sides.

3 Beat butter and sugar in small bowl with electric mixer until just combined. Add eggs one at a time, beating until just combined between additions. Add the butter mixture to fruit mixture; mix well. Stir in sifted flour and spice, then nuts.

4 Spread mixture into pan. Bake about 3 hours. Brush top of cake with extra liqueur. Cover hot cake tightly with foil, turn cake upside down; cool in pan.

5 Combine sugar and the water in small saucepan; stir over heat until sugar is dissolved. Boil, uncovered, 1 minute, cool syrup.

6 Place cake top-side down on board. Brush top of cake with some of the syrup.

7 Knead icing until smooth, on surface dusted with sifted icing sugar. Roll out icing until large enough to cover top of cake. Lift icing onto the cake; smooth with hands, trim excess icing. Stand 3 hours or overnight until firm.

8 Place cutter gently on cake to use as a guide. Brush the icing inside the cutter with a little syrup, sprinkle with cachous; remove cutter. Decorate sides of cake with ribbon.

Line base and sides of pan with two layers of brown and two layers of baking paper.

Brush icing inside cutter with a little syrup then sprinkle with cachous.

gluten-free fruit and almond loaves

PREPARATION TIME 35 MINUTES (PLUS STANDING TIME) COOKING TIME 2 HOURS MAKES 2

Check all labels to ensure the products do not contain gluten.

1kg mixed dried fruit

1 tablespoon finely grated orange rind

⅔ cup (160ml) sweet sherry

150g butter, softened

⅔ cup (150g) firmly packed dark brown sugar

4 eggs

100g marzipan, chopped coarsely

1 small apple (130g), grated coarsely

¾ cup (100g) almond meal

1¼ cups (185g) gluten-free plain flour

1 cup (160g) blanched almonds

¼ cup (60ml) sweet sherry, extra

1 Combine fruit, rind and sherry in large bowl; mix well, cover tightly with plastic wrap. Store mixture in cool, dark place overnight or for several days, stirring every day.

2 Preheat oven to 150°C/130°C fan-forced. Line bases and sides of two 9cm x 21cm loaf pans with two layers of baking paper, bringing paper 5cm above sides.

3 Beat butter and sugar in small bowl with electric mixer until just combined. Add eggs one at a time, beating until just combined between additions. Add butter mixture to fruit mixture; mix well. Stir in marzipan, apple, almond meal and sifted flour.

4 Spread mixture into pans; decorate with nuts. Bake about 2 hours or until cooked. Brush hot loaves with extra sherry; cover with foil; cool in pans.

golden glacé fruit cake

PREPARATION TIME 35 MINUTES   **COOKING TIME** 2 HOURS (PLUS COOLING TIME)

250g butter, softened

1 cup (220g) caster sugar

4 eggs

1 cup (190g) mixed dried fruit

¾ cup (185g) quartered glacé cherries

½ cup (125g) chopped glacé apricots

⅓ cup (85g) chopped glacé peaches

½ cup (115g) chopped glacé pineapple

¾ cup (125g) blanched almonds, roasted, halved

1 cup (150g) plain flour

1 cup (150g) self-raising flour

¼ cup (60ml) Cointreau

¼ cup (60ml) apricot jam

1 Preheat oven to 160°C/140°C fan-forced. Grease deep 22cm-round cake pan or deep 19cm-square cake pan, line base and side(s) with three layers baking paper, extending paper 5cm above side(s).

2 Beat butter and sugar in large bowl with electric mixer until changed to a lighter colour. Add eggs, one at a time, beating until just combined between additions. Stir in fruit, nuts, sifted flours, liqueur and jam.

3 Spread cake mixture into pan; bake about 2 hours. Cover hot cake with foil; cool in pan.

festive fruit and nut cake

PREPARATION TIME 20 MINUTES **COOKING TIME** 1 HOURS 45 MINUTES

½ cup (115g) coarsely chopped glacé pineapple

½ cup (125g) coarsely chopped glacé apricots

1½ cups (250g) seeded dried dates

½ cup (110g) red glacé cherries

½ cup (110g) green glacé cherries

1 cup (170g) brazil nuts

½ cup (75g) macadamia nuts

2 eggs

½ cup (110g) firmly packed brown sugar

1 tablespoon dark rum

100g butter, melted

⅓ cup (50g) plain flour

¼ cup (35g) self-raising flour

FRUIT AND NUT TOPPING

⅓ cup (75g) coarsely chopped glacé pineapple

¼ cup (55g) red glacé cherries, halved

¼ cup (55g) green glacé cherries, halved

¼ cup (40g) brazil nuts

¼ cup (35g) macadamia nuts

TOFFEE TOPPING

½ cup (110g) caster sugar

¼ cup (60ml) water

1 Preheat oven to 150°C/130°C fan-forced.

2 Grease 20cm-ring pan; line base and side with baking paper, extending paper 5cm above side.

3 Combine fruit and nuts in large bowl.

4 Beat eggs and sugar in small bowl with electric mixer until thick. Add rum, butter and sifted flours; beat until just combined. Stir egg mixture into fruit mixture. Press mixture firmly into pan.

5 Make fruit and nut topping. Gently press topping evenly over cake mixture; bake, covered, 1 hour. Uncover; bake about 45 minutes. Stand cake in pan 10 minutes.

6 Make toffee topping. Turn cake, top-side up, onto wire rack; drizzle with toffee topping.

FRUIT AND NUT TOPPING Combine ingredients in medium bowl.

TOFFEE TOPPING Combine ingredients in small saucepan, stir over heat without boiling until sugar dissolves. Bring to a boil; simmer, uncovered, without stirring, about 10 minutes or until mixture is golden. Remove from heat; stand until bubbles subside before using.

TIP This cake can be baked in two 8cm x 26cm bar cake pans. Line bases and sides with baking paper, extending paper 5cm above long sides. Bake, covered, in 150°C/130°C fan-forced oven 1 hour; uncover, bake about 30 minutes.

celebration fruit cake

PREPARATION TIME 20 MINUTES (PLUS STANDING TIME)   **COOKING TIME** 3 HOURS 30 MINUTES (PLUS COOLING TIME)

3 cups (500g) sultanas

1¾ cups (300g) raisins, halved

1¾ cups (300g) dried seedless dates, chopped finely

1 cup (150g) dried currants

⅔ cup (110g) mixed peel

⅔ cup (150g) glacé cherries, halved

¼ cup (55g) coarsely chopped glacé pineapple

¼ cup (60g) coarsely chopped glacé apricots

½ cup (125ml) dark rum

250g butter, softened

1 cup (220g) firmly packed brown sugar

5 eggs

1½ cups (225g) plain flour

⅓ cup (50g) self-raising flour

1 teaspoon mixed spice

2 tablespoons dark rum, extra

1 Combine fruit and rum in large bowl; mix well, cover tightly with plastic wrap. Store mixture in cool, dark place overnight or up to a week, stirring every day.

2 Preheat oven to 150°C/130°C fan-forced. Line deep 22cm-round cake pan with three thicknesses of baking paper, extending paper 5cm above side.

3 Beat butter and sugar in small bowl with electric mixer until just combined. Add eggs, one at a time, beating only until combined between additions.

4 Add butter mixture to fruit mixture; mix well. Mix in sifted dry ingredients; spread mixture evenly into pan. Bake about 3½ hours.

5 Brush cake with extra rum. Cover hot cake with foil; cool in pan.

sweet dishes ❄ desserts

lemon lime sorbet

PREPARATION TIME 20 MINUTES **COOKING TIME** 10 MINUTES (PLUS FREEZING TIME) **SERVES** 8

2 tablespoons finely grated
lemon rind

1 tablespoon finely grated lime rind

1 cup (220g) caster sugar

2½ cups (625ml) water

½ cup (125ml) lemon juice

¼ cup (60ml) lime juice

1 egg white

1 Stir rinds, sugar and the water in medium saucepan over high heat until sugar dissolves; simmer without stirring, uncovered, 5 minutes. Transfer to large heatproof jug, cool; stir in juices.

2 Pour sorbet mixture into loaf pan, cover with foil; freeze 3 hours or overnight.

3 Process mixture with egg white until smooth. Return to loaf pan, cover; freeze until firm.

passionfruit sorbet

PREPARATION TIME 20 MINUTES **COOKING TIME** 10 MINUTES (PLUS FREEZING TIME) **SERVES** 8

*You need 12 medium passionfruit
for this recipe.*

1 cup (250ml) passionfruit pulp

1 cup (220g) caster sugar

2½ cups (625ml) water

¼ cup (60ml) lemon juice

2 egg whites

1 Strain pulp into small bowl. Reserve seeds and juice.

2 Stir sugar and the water in medium saucepan over high heat until sugar dissolves; simmer without stirring, uncovered, 5 minutes. Transfer to large heatproof jug, cool; stir in juices.

3 Pour sorbet mixture into loaf pan, cover with foil; freeze 3 hours or overnight.

4 Process mixture with egg whites until smooth; stir in reserved seeds. Return to loaf pan, cover; freeze until firm.

raspberry sorbet

PREPARATION TIME 20 MINUTES **COOKING TIME** 10 MINUTES (PLUS FREEZING TIME) **SERVES** 8

360g raspberries

1 cup (220g) caster sugar

2½ cups (625ml) water

1 tablespoon lemon juice

1 egg white

1 Press raspberries through sieve into small bowl; discard seeds.

2 Stir sugar and the water in medium saucepan over high heat until sugar dissolves; simmer without stirring, uncovered, 5 minutes. Transfer to large heatproof jug, cool; stir in raspberry pulp and juice.

3 Pour sorbet mixture into loaf pan, cover with foil; freeze 3 hours or overnight.

4 Process mixture with egg white until smooth. Return to loaf pan, cover; freeze until firm.

roast nectarine tart

PREPARATION TIME 40 MINUTES (PLUS REFRIGERATION TIME) COOKING TIME 35 MINUTES (PLUS COOLING TIME) SERVES 8

Pastry case, crème patissiere and nectarines can be made a day ahead. Assemble close to serving. We used very small nectarines for this recipe. If larger nectarines are used, quarter them.

1⅔ cups (250g) plain flour

⅔ cup (110g) icing sugar

125g cold butter, chopped

1 egg yolk

1 tablespoon iced water, approximately

1.6kg small firm nectarines, halved

½ cup (110g) firmly packed brown sugar

¼ cup (60ml) orange juice

CRÈME PATISSIERE

1 cup (250ml) cream

1½ cups (375ml) milk

½ cup (110g) caster sugar

1 vanilla bean, split lengthways

2 eggs

¼ cup (35g) cornflour

90g butter, chopped

1 Process flour, icing sugar, butter and egg yolk until combined. Add enough of the water to make ingredients cling together.

2 Knead pastry gently on lightly floured surface until smooth. Wrap pastry in plastic, refrigerate 30 minutes. Roll pastry between sheets of baking paper until large enough to line base and sides of 19cm x 27cm rectangular loose-based flan tin.

3 Carefully lift pastry into tin, press into sides. Place flan tin on oven tray; refrigerate 30 minutes.

4 Preheat oven to 180°C/160°C fan-forced.

5 Cover pastry with baking paper, fill with dried beans or rice. Bake 10 minutes; remove paper and beans. Bake further 10 minutes or until browned lightly. Cool.

6 Increase oven temperature to 220°C/200°C fan-forced.

7 Place nectarines in large baking dish; sprinkle with brown sugar and juice. Roast, uncovered, about 20 minutes or until nectarines are soft.

8 Make crème patissiere.

9 Spoon crème patissiere into pastry case; refrigerate tart about 30 minutes or until firm. Top with nectarines.

CRÈME PATISSIERE Bring cream, milk, sugar and vanilla bean to a boil in medium saucepan. Whisk eggs in large bowl, whisk in sifted cornflour. Gradually whisk in hot milk mixture. Strain mixture into same pan; stir over heat until mixture boils and thickens. Remove from heat; whisk in butter. Cover surface with plastic wrap; cool.

chocolate jaffa tart

PREPARATION TIME 30 MINUTES (PLUS REFRIGERATION TIME) **COOKING TIME** 55 MINUTES (PLUS COOLING TIME) **SERVES** 8

1½ cups (225g) plain flour

¼ cup (40g) icing sugar

125g cold unsalted butter, chopped

2 egg yolks

2 teaspoons iced water

3 eggs

1 tablespoon finely grated orange rind

⅔ cup (160ml) thickened cream

¾ cup (165g) caster sugar

60g dark chocolate, melted

2 tablespoons cocoa powder

2 tablespoons Grand Marnier

140g dark chocolate, chopped coarsely

¼ cup (60ml) thickened cream, extra

20 Ferrero Rocher chocolates, halved

1 Grease 24cm-round loose-based flan tin.

2 Blend or process flour, icing sugar and butter until crumbly. Add egg yolks and the water, process until ingredients just come together. Knead pastry on floured surface until smooth. Cover with plastic wrap; refrigerate 30 minutes.

3 Roll pastry between sheets of baking paper until large enough to line tin; lift pastry into tin. Press into side; trim edge. Cover; refrigerate 30 minutes.

4 Preheat oven to 200°C/180°C fan-forced.

5 Cover pastry with baking paper; fill with dried beans or rice. Place on oven tray; bake 10 minutes. Remove paper and beans. Bake further 10 minutes or until pastry is browned lightly; cool. Reduce oven temperature to 180°C/160°C fan-forced.

6 Whisk eggs, rind, cream, caster sugar, melted chocolate, sifted cocoa and liqueur in medium bowl until combined.

7 Pour chocolate mixture into pastry case. Bake about 30 minutes or until filling is set; cool.

8 Place chopped chocolate and extra cream in small saucepan; stir over low heat until smooth. Spread warm chocolate mixture over top of cold tart; refrigerate until set. Just before serving, decorate with Ferrero Rocher halves.

raspberry and white chocolate cheesecake

PREPARATION TIME 30 MINUTES (PLUS REFRIGERATION TIME)
COOKING TIME 1 HOUR 30 MINUTES (PLUS COOLING TIME) **SERVES 10**

200g plain chocolate biscuits

90g white eating chocolate, chopped finely

80g butter, melted

½ cup (125ml) cream

200g white eating chocolate, chopped finely, extra

1 cup (250g) mascarpone cheese

250g cream cheese

½ cup (110g) caster sugar

3 eggs

2 egg whites

360g fresh raspberries

1 Blend or process biscuits until fine. Add chocolate and butter; process until just combined.

2 Press crumb mixture evenly over base and side of 25cm springform pan. Cover; refrigerate 30 minutes.

3 Preheat oven to 150°C/130°C fan-forced.

4 Place cream in small saucepan, bring to a boil, pour over extra chocolate in small bowl; stir until melted, cool 10 minutes.

5 Beat cheeses and sugar in medium bowl with electric mixer until smooth; beat in eggs, one at a time, then chocolate mixture, beating until just combined.

6 Beat egg whites in clean small bowl with electric mixer until soft peaks form. Fold half the berries, then the egg whites into chocolate mixture, in two batches.

7 Place pan on oven tray; pour cheesecake mixture into pan. Bake about 1½ hours or until just firm. Cool in oven with door ajar.

8 Refrigerate cheesecake 3 hours or overnight. Remove from pan just before serving. Top cheesecake with remaining raspberries and dust with sifted icing sugar, if desired.

raspberry toffee ice-cream cake

PREPARATION TIME 15 MINUTES (PLUS REFRIGERATION TIME) **SERVES 12**

1 litre vanilla ice-cream

1 litre raspberry sorbet
(or other fruit flavour)

1 litre english toffee ice-cream

240g fresh raspberries

1 Line deep 19cm-square cake pan with plastic wrap; cover base and extend over sides.

2 Soften vanilla ice-cream slightly. Spoon into pan, press into an even layer with the back of a spoon. Cover; freeze about 1 hour or until firm.

3 Spoon sorbet over ice cream; press firmly to form an even layer. Cover; freeze about 1 hour or until firm.

4 Soften toffee ice-cream slightly, spread over sorbet as above. Cover, freeze about 6 hours or until firm.

5 Turn cake onto serving plate, remove plastic; top with raspberries.

chocolate roulade with coffee cream

PREPARATION TIME 20 MINUTES **COOKING TIME** 10 MINUTES (PLUS COOLING AND REFRIGERATION TIME) **SERVES 8**

Tia Maria, Kahlua and crème de caçao are all coffee-flavoured liqueurs; any one of them can be used in this recipe.

200g dark eating chocolate, chopped coarsely

¼ cup (60ml) hot water

1 tablespoon instant coffee granules

4 eggs, separated

½ cup (110g) caster sugar

1 tablespoon caster sugar, extra

1 teaspoon hot water, extra

300ml thickened cream

2 tablespoons coffee-flavoured liqueur

1 tablespoon icing sugar

1 Preheat oven to 180°C/160°C fan-forced. Grease 25cm x 30cm swiss roll pan; line base with baking paper.

2 Combine chocolate, the water and half the coffee in large heatproof bowl. Stir over large saucepan of simmering water until smooth; remove from heat.

3 Beat egg yolks and caster sugar in small bowl with electric mixer until thick and creamy; fold egg mixture into warm chocolate mixture.

4 Meanwhile, beat egg whites in small bowl with electric mixer until soft peaks form; fold egg whites into chocolate mixture, in two batches. Spread into pan; bake about 10 minutes.

5 Place a piece of baking paper cut the same size as swiss roll pan on bench; sprinkle evenly with extra caster sugar. Turn cake onto sugared paper, peel lining paper away; use serrated knife to cut away crisp edges from all sides of cake. Cover cake with tea towel; cool.

6 Dissolve remaining coffee in the extra water in small bowl. Add cream, liqueur and icing sugar; beat with electric mixer until firm peaks form. Spread cake evenly with cream mixture. Roll cake, from long side, by lifting paper and using it to guide the roll into log shape. Cover roll; refrigerate 30 minutes before serving.

hints These two desserts are perfect solutions for the busy Christmas cook. You can prepare the ice-cream cake up to a week ahead, freeze it and cover with foil. The fat content of ice-cream varies from product to product; the lower the fat, the quicker it melts, and vice versa. For this reason, you may not achieve perfectly even layers in your cake. Chocolate roulade is a fantastic choice for a quick dessert; make the cake a day before serving to save time. If you're not a coffee lover, substitute something different for the coffee liqueur; perhaps a splash of framboise (a raspberry-flavoured liqueur) and some fresh raspberries…yum.

vanilla pear almond cake

PREPARATION TIME 30 MINS (PLUS COOLING TIME) **COOKING TIME** 1 HOUR 15 MINS **SERVES 8**

8 small corella pears (800g)

1 vanilla bean

2½ cups (625ml) water

1 cup (220g) caster sugar

1 strip lemon rind

125g butter, chopped

¾ cup (165g) caster sugar, extra

3 eggs

⅔ cup (160g) sour cream

⅔ cup (100g) plain flour

⅔ cup (100g) self-raising flour

¼ cup (40g) roasted almonds, chopped finely

40g dark eating chocolate, chopped finely

½ cup (60g) almond meal

1 Peel pears, leaving stems intact.

2 Split vanilla bean in half lengthways; scrape out seeds. Combine vanilla bean, seeds, the water, sugar and rind in small saucepan. Stir over heat until the sugar is dissolved.

3 Add pears; simmer, covered, 20 minutes or until pears are almost tender. Remove pears from syrup. Boil syrup, uncovered, until reduced to 1 cup (250ml); cool. Trim bases of pears to sit flat.

4 Preheat oven to 160°C/140°C fan-forced. Grease 26cm springform pan; line base with baking paper. Insert base of springform pan upside down to make the cake easier to remove.

5 Beat butter and extra sugar in small bowl with electric mixer until smooth. Add eggs, one at a time, beating until just combined. Add cream; beat until just combined. Stir in 2 tablespoons of the syrup. Transfer mixture to large bowl. Stir in sifted flours, nuts, chocolate and meal.

6 Spread mixture into pan; arrange pears around pan edge, gently pushing to the bottom of pan. Bake about 50 minutes. Remove ring from pan.

7 Serve cake warm or cool with remaining syrup.

sweet dishes ❄ puddings

three-in-one Christmas mix

One quantity of this basic fruit mixture recipe makes enough for the following three Christmas recipes. The mixture can be made a month before required, and stored in a cool, dark place – your refrigerator is ideal. Ideally, the ingredients shown below as "chopped" should all be cut to a similar size, about that of a sultana. Grand Marnier liqueur was used in keeping with the citrus content of the mixture (you can use any citrus-flavoured liqueur), but it can be substituted with rum, sherry or brandy.

basic fruit mixture

PREPARATION TIME 45 MINUTES (PLUS STANDING TIME)

6 cups (1kg) sultanas

2½ cups (375g) dried currants

2¼ cups (425g) raisins, chopped

1½ cups (250g) seeded dried dates, chopped

1½ cups (250g) seeded prunes, chopped

1¼ cups (250g) glacé cherries, quartered

½ cup (125g) glacé apricots, chopped

½ cup (115g) glacé pineapple, chopped

½ cup (115g) glacé ginger, chopped

¾ cup (120g) mixed peel

3 medium apples (450g), peeled, grated

⅔ cup (240g) fig jam

2 tablespoons finely grated orange rind

¼ cup (60ml) lemon juice

2 cups (440g) firmly packed brown sugar

1 tablespoon mixed spice

1⅓ cups (330ml) Grand Marnier

1 Combine ingredients in large bowl; cover tightly with plastic wrap. Store mixture in cool, dark place for a month (or longer) before using; stir mixture every two or three days.

THREE-IN-ONE CHRISTMAS MIX

Christmas pudding

PREPARATION TIME 15 MINUTES COOKING TIME 4 HOURS (PLUS STANDING TIME) SERVES 12-14

You need a 60cm square of unbleached calico for the pudding cloth. If calico has not been used before, soak in cold water overnight; next day, boil it for 20 minutes then rinse in cold water.

¼ quantity basic fruit mixture (page 110)

250g butter, melted, cooled

3 eggs, beaten lightly

4 cups (280g) stale breadcrumbs

¼ cup (35g) plain flour

1 Combine basic fruit mixture in large bowl with butter and eggs then breadcrumbs and flour.

2 Fill large boiler three-quarters full of hot water, cover; bring to a boil. Have ready 2.5 metres of kitchen string and an extra ½ cup plain flour. Wearing thick rubber gloves, put pudding cloth in boiling water; boil 1 minute; squeeze excess water from cloth. Working quickly, spread hot cloth on bench, rub flour into centre of cloth to cover an area about 40cm in diameter, leaving flour a little thicker in centre of cloth where "skin" on the pudding needs to be thickest.

3 Place pudding mixture in centre of cloth. Gather cloth evenly around mixture, avoiding any deep pleats; then pat into round shape. Tie cloth tightly with string as close to mixture as possible. Pull ends of cloth tightly to ensure pudding is as round and firm as possible. Knot two pairs of corners together to make pudding easier to remove.

4 Lower pudding into boiling water; tie free ends of string to handles of boiler to suspend pudding. Cover with tight-fitting lid; boil rapidly 4 hours, replenishing water as necessary to maintain level.

5 Untie pudding from handles; place wooden spoon through knotted calico loops to lift pudding from water. Do not put pudding on bench; suspend from spoon by placing over rungs of upturned stool or wedging handle in a drawer. Pudding must be suspended freely. Twist wet ends of cloth around string to avoid them touching pudding. If pudding has been cooked correctly, cloth will start to dry in patches within a few minutes; hang 10 minutes.

6 Place pudding on board; cut string, carefully peel back cloth. Turn pudding onto a plate then carefully peel cloth away completely; cool. Stand at least 20 minutes or until skin darkens and pudding becomes firm before serving.

TIP For tips on how to store and reheat this pudding, see *steamed Christmas pudding* recipe (page 122).

moist Christmas cake

PREPARATION TIME 15 MINUTES **COOKING TIME** 3 HOURS (PLUS COOLING TIME)

½ quantity basic fruit mixture
(page 110)

250g butter, melted, cooled

5 eggs, beaten lightly

2½ cups (375g) plain flour

2 tablespoons Grand Marnier

1 Preheat oven to 150°C/130°C fan-forced. Line base and sides of deep 22cm-square cake pan with one thickness brown paper and two thicknesses baking paper, extending papers 5cm above sides.

2 Combine basic fruit mixture in large bowl with butter and eggs; add sifted flour in two batches.

3 Spread mixture into pan; level top with spatula. Bake about 3 hours. Brush with liqueur; cover hot cake in pan with foil, cool in pan.

TIP Can be made three months ahead and stored in an airtight container under refrigeration.

fruit mince slice

PREPARATION TIME 10 MINUTES **COOKING TIME** 25 MINUTES

2 sheets ready-rolled puff pastry

¼ quantity basic fruit mixture
(page 110)

1 egg white, beaten lightly

1 tablespoon caster sugar

1 Preheat oven to 220°C/200°C fan-forced. Grease 20cm x 30cm lamington pan.

2 Cut one pastry sheet large enough to cover base of pan. Using fork, prick pastry all over several times. Place 19cm x 29cm slice pan on top of pastry to prevent pastry rising during cooking.

3 Bake pastry about 10 minutes or until pastry is browned lightly and crisp.

4 Remove slice pan; spread fruit mixture evenly over pastry.

5 Cut remaining pastry sheet large enough to cover fruit mixture. Brush pastry with egg white, sprinkle with sugar; score pastry in crosshatch pattern. Bake about 15 minutes or until pastry is browned.

hints Our basic fruit mix makes Christmas baking a breeze. Why choose between making a cake or a pudding this year, when you can make both; these recipes will make mouths water and tummies sing with delight. You can mix and match the ingredients to your heart's content; maybe you don't feel like fig jam this year, use a delicious plum jam instead; you can substitute whisky for Grand Marnier if you don't want the citrus hit. We think this mixture is fantastic; it's versatile and yummy. How about using any leftover mix to make delicious fruit mince pies; serve them with coffee and your guests are sure to be impressed.

irish pudding cake

PREPARATION TIME 25 MINUTES (PLUS STANDING TIME) **COOKING TIME** 3 HOURS (PLUS COOLING TIME) **SERVES** 12

1½ cups (250g) seeded dried dates, chopped coarsely

1¼ cups (200g) seeded prunes, chopped coarsely

1½ cups (225g) raisins, chopped coarsely

1 cup (150g) dried currants

¾ cup (125g) sultanas

1 large apple (200g), grated coarsely

1½ cups (375ml) irish whiskey

1¼ cups (275g) firmly packed dark brown sugar

185g butter, softened

3 eggs, beaten lightly

½ cup (50g) hazelnut meal

1½ cups (225g) plain flour

1 teaspoon ground nutmeg

½ teaspoon ground ginger

½ teaspoon ground cloves

½ teaspoon bicarbonate of soda

1 Combine fruit and 1 cup of the whiskey in large bowl, cover tightly with plastic wrap; stand at room temperature overnight.

2 Preheat oven to 120°C/100°C fan-forced. Line deep 20cm-round cake pan with two thicknesses baking paper, extending paper 5cm above side.

3 Combine remaining whiskey and ½ cup of the sugar in small saucepan. Stir over heat until sugar dissolves; bring to a boil; cool syrup 20 minutes.

4 Meanwhile, beat butter and remaining sugar in small bowl with electric mixer until just combined (do not overbeat). Add eggs, one at a time, beating until combined between additions. Add butter mixture to fruit mixture; stir in hazelnut meal, sifted dry ingredients and ½ cup of the cooled syrup.

5 Spread mixture into pan. Bake about 3 hours. Brush cake with reheated remaining syrup, cover with foil; cool in pan.

TIPS If your dilemma is whether to make a Christmas cake or pudding, this recipe is the best of both worlds because it's just as delicious served hot as a pudding or cold as a cake. It's not necessary to make it ages in advance, either: starting to prepare it a day or so ahead is just fine. It will keep, covered, in the refrigerator for up to a month. Although the inclusion of irish whiskey makes it authentic, scotch, dark rum or brandy are fine substitutes.

frozen chocolate fruit cake pudding

PREPARATION TIME 40 MINUTES (PLUS STANDING, REFRIGERATION AND FREEZING TIME)
COOKING TIME 10 MINUTES SERVES 10

½ cup (95g) coarsely chopped dried figs

¼ cup (40g) coarsely chopped raisins

¼ cup (50g) coarsely chopped dried prunes

¼ cup (60g) coarsely chopped glacé cherries

4 fresh dates (100g), seeded, chopped coarsely

2 teaspoons finely grated orange rind

½ cup (125ml) brandy

125g butter

½ cup (75g) plain flour

½ cup (110g) firmly packed brown sugar

1 cup (250ml) milk

600ml thickened cream

⅔ cup (220g) chocolate hazelnut spread

1 teaspoon ground nutmeg

1 teaspoon ground cinnamon

4 egg yolks

⅓ cup (50g) roasted hazelnuts, chopped coarsely

200g dark eating chocolate, chopped finely

200g dark eating chocolate, melted

1 Combine fruit, rind and brandy in large bowl. Cover tightly with plastic wrap; store in a cool, dark place overnight or up to a week, stirring every day.

2 Line 17.5cm, 1.75-litre (7-cup) pudding basin with plastic wrap, extending plastic 5cm over edge.

3 Melt butter in medium saucepan, add flour; stir over heat until bubbling. Remove from heat; stir in sugar then milk and half the cream. Stir over heat until mixture boils and thickens. Transfer to large bowl; stir in spread, spices and yolks. Cover surface of mixture with plastic wrap; refrigerate 1 hour.

4 Stir in fruit mixture, nuts and chopped chocolate. Beat remaining cream in small bowl with electric mixer until soft peaks form, fold into pudding mixture. Spoon mixture into basin, tap basin lightly to remove air bubbles. Cover with foil; freeze 3 hours or overnight.

5 Turn pudding onto tray; remove plastic wrap, return pudding to freezer.

6 Cut a 35cm circle from a piece of paper to use as a guide; cover paper with plastic wrap. Spread melted chocolate over plastic wrap then quickly drape plastic, chocolate-side down, over pudding. Quickly smooth with hands, avoiding deep pleats in the plastic. Freeze until firm. Peel away plastic; trim away excess chocolate. Serve with a selection of fresh and frosted seasonal fruit.

allergy-free pudding

PREPARATION TIME 20 MINUTES **COOKING TIME** 6 HOURS **SERVES** 12

This recipe is gluten-free, contains no dairy products or eggs, and makes either one pudding or one cake (see recipe, below).

2¼ cups (360g) sultanas

1½ cups (250g) chopped raisins

½ cup (75g) dried currants

1½ cups (250g) chopped seeded dates

1½ cups (375ml) water

½ cup (125ml) orange juice

2 tablespoons honey

1 cup (200g) firmly packed brown sugar

185g dairy-free margarine

1 cup (125g) soy flour

1 cup (150g) rice flour

1 teaspoon cream of tartar

½ teaspoon bicarbonate of soda

2 teaspoons mixed spice

1 cup (125g) almond meal

1 Combine fruit, the water, juice, honey, sugar and margarine in large saucepan. Stir over heat, without boiling, until margarine melts. Transfer mixture to large heatproof bowl; cool.

2 Grease 2.25-litre (9-cup) pudding steamer, line base with baking paper.

3 Stir sifted dry ingredients and almond meal into fruit mixture.

4 Spoon mixture into steamer, cover pudding with greased foil; secure with lid or kitchen string. Place steamer in large saucepan with enough boiling water to come halfway up side of steamer; simmer, covered, about 6 hours, replenishing water as necessary to maintain level.

allergy-free cake

PREPARATION TIME 30 MINUTES **COOKING TIME** 2 HOURS 30 MINUTES (PLUS COOLING TIME)

1 Preheat oven to 150°C/130°C fan-forced. Grease deep 19cm-square cake pan, line base and sides with two layers baking paper, extending paper 5cm above sides.

2 Complete cake mixture following instructions as per allergy-free pudding, then spread mixture into pan; bake about 2½ hours, covering loosely with foil after 1 hour.

3 Cover hot cake tightly with foil; cool in pan.

steamed Christmas pudding

PREPARATION TIME 25 MINUTES   COOKING TIME 4 HOURS 15 MINUTES (PLUS COOLING TIME)   SERVES 12

3 cups (450g) chopped
mixed dried fruit

¾ cup (120g) finely chopped
dried seedless dates

¾ cup (120g) finely
chopped raisins

¾ cup (180ml) water

1 cup (220g) firmly
packed brown sugar

100g butter, chopped

1 teaspoon bicarbonate of soda

2 eggs, beaten lightly

¾ cup (110g) plain flour

¾ cup (110g) self-raising flour

1 teaspoon mixed spice

½ teaspoon ground cinnamon

2 tablespoons dark rum

1 Combine fruit, the water, sugar and butter in medium saucepan. Stir over medium heat until butter melts and sugar dissolves; simmer, uncovered, 6 minutes. Stir in soda. Transfer mixture to large bowl; cool to room temperature.

2 Stir in eggs, sifted dry ingredients and rum.

3 Grease 2-litre (8-cup) pudding steamer; spoon mixture into steamer. Top with pleated baking paper and foil (to allow pudding to expand as it cooks); secure with kitchen string or lid.

4 Place pudding in large boiler with enough boiling water to come halfway up side of steamer. Cover with tight-fitting lid, boil for 4 hours, replenishing water as necessary to maintain level. Stand pudding 10 minutes before serving.

TO STORE PUDDING Allow pudding to come to room temperature then wrap pudding in plastic wrap; refrigerate in cleaned steamer, or seal tightly in freezer bag or airtight container. Pudding can be stored in refrigerator up to two months or frozen up to 12 months.

TO REHEAT Thaw frozen pudding three days in refrigerator; remove from refrigerator 12 hours before reheating. Remove from plastic wrap and return to steamer. Steam 2 hours following instructions in step 4.

TO REHEAT IN MICROWAVE OVEN Reheat up to four single serves at once. Cover with plastic wrap; microwave on HIGH (100%) up to 1 minute per serve. To reheat whole pudding, cover with plastic wrap; microwave on MEDIUM (55%) about 15 minutes or until hot.

boiled Christmas pudding

PREPARATION TIME 30 MINUTES (PLUS STANDING TIME) **COOKING TIME** 6 HOURS (PLUS COOLING TIME) **SERVES** 12-14

You need a 60cm square of unbleached calico for the pudding cloth. If calico has not been used before, soak in cold water overnight; next day, boil it for 20 minutes then rinse in cold water.

1½ cups (225g) raisins

1½ cups (240g) sultanas

1 cup (150g) dried currants

¾ cup (120g) mixed peel

1 teaspoon finely grated lemon rind

2 tablespoons lemon juice

2 tablespoons brandy

250g butter, softened

2 cups (440g) firmly packed brown sugar

5 eggs

1¼ cups (185g) plain flour

½ teaspoon ground nutmeg

½ teaspoon mixed spice

4 cups (280g) stale breadcrumbs

1 Combine fruit, rind, juice and brandy in large bowl; mix well. Cover tightly with plastic wrap; store in a cool, dark place overnight or up to a week, stirring every day.

2 Beat butter and sugar in large bowl with electric mixer only until combined. Beat in eggs, one at a time, beat only until combined between each addition. Add butter mixture to fruit mixture then sifted dry ingredients and breadcrumbs; mix well.

3 Boil pudding about 6 hours, replenishing water as necessary to maintain level.

TIP See *Christmas pudding* recipe, page 113, for detailed instructions on preparing and boiling pudding.

creamy custard sauce

PREPARATION TIME 15 MINUTES
COOKING TIME 5 MINUTES MAKES ABOUT 1 LITRE (4 CUPS)

½ cup (110g) caster sugar

1 cup (250ml) water

4 egg yolks

300ml thickened cream, whipped lightly

1 Combine sugar and the water in small saucepan; stir over medium heat, without boiling, until sugar is dissolved. Bring to a boil; simmer, uncovered, until sugar syrup is reduced to about ½ cup (125ml).

2 Beat egg yolks in small bowl with electric mixer until thick and creamy. Gradually beat in hot sugar syrup in a thin stream; beat until mixture is thick and creamy. Fold in cream. Refrigerate until ready to serve.

TIP Sauce can be made two days ahead; store, covered, in refrigerator.

orange liqueur butter

PREPARATION TIME 10 MINUTES SERVES 8

125g soft unsalted butter

¼ cup (40g) icing sugar

1 teaspoon grated orange rind

2 tablespoons orange juice

1 tablespoon orange-flavoured liqueur

1 Beat butter in small bowl with electric mixer until soft and creamy. Beat in the sifted icing sugar and rind, then the juice and liqueur. Refrigerate until required.

TIP Butter can be made three days ahead; keep, covered, in refrigerator. Butter can also be frozen for up to one month.

hard sauce

PREPARATION TIME 15 MINUTES SERVES 12

250g soft butter

2 cups (320g) pure icing sugar, sifted

¼ cup (60ml) cream

⅓ cup (80ml) brandy

1 Beat butter and icing sugar in small bowl with electric mixer until as white as possible; beat in cream and brandy.

TIP Sauce can be made a week ahead; store, covered, in refrigerator. Sauce can also be frozen for up to one month.

liqueur custard

PREPARATION TIME 10 MINUTES
COOKING TIME 25 MINUTES (PLUS STANDING TIME)
MAKES ABOUT 3½ CUPS

2 cups (500ml) milk

300ml thickened cream

1 vanilla bean, split

6 egg yolks

⅓ cup (75g) caster sugar

2 tablespoons orange-flavoured liqueur

1 Combine milk, cream and vanilla bean in medium saucepan; heat until just below boiling point. Stand 15 minutes; remove vanilla bean.

2 Beat egg yolks and sugar in small bowl with electric mixer until thick and creamy. Gradually whisk hot milk mixture into egg mixture.

3 Return milk mixture to pan, stir over low heat, without boiling, until custard thickens and coats the back of a metal spoon. Stir in liqueur.

little gift cakes

PREPARATION TIME 1 HOUR 30 MINUTES (PLUS STANDING TIME) **MAKES 9**

1 x 19cm-square fruit cake
2 x 500g packets soft icing
icing sugar, for dusting
food colourings
¾ cup (180ml) apricot jam, warmed, sieved
ribbons and decorations

1 Cut cake into nine even pieces; cover to keep airtight.

2 Knead icing until smooth on surface dusted with sifted icing sugar. Divide icing so that you have nine pieces in total. Tint each piece by kneading in one of the colourings – leave some pieces uncoloured if white icing is desired. Wrap tinted pieces individually in plastic wrap until ready to use.

3 Brush top and sides of cake evenly with jam just before it is ready to be covered with icing. Roll out icing between sheets of baking paper until large enough to cover top and sides of cake. Lift icing onto cake, then lightly mould icing over cake with dusted hands; trim edges neatly.

4 Repeat with remaining icing and cakes. Icing scraps can be cut to make decorative shapes; secure shapes to cakes with a little more jam. Decorate cakes with ribbons and decorations.

TIPS To give as gifts, the cakes can be placed on pieces of thick cardboard, measuring about 9cm-square, covered with special foil or glossy gift paper. Gift cakes can be made a month ahead; store in an airtight container at room temperature.
For bold coloured icings, use powdered food colourings, available from cake decorating suppliers and some health food stores. Mixing the powder with a very small amount of hot water before being kneaded into the soft icing gives a better result. Liquid colourings can be used for paler colours.

hints Truffles are a cook's secret pleasure: they look splendidly impressive but are actually quite effortless to make. Basically a round of chilled flavoured ganache rolled in melted milk, dark or white chocolate with, perhaps, cocoa, coconut, chopped nuts or citrus rind, a truffle is refrigerated until it's set then presented en masse or singly, with coffee or as a gift. It is thought to have been named by French confectioners who thought it bore visual similarity to the rare black mushroom, and it's true that the two are equally luxurious and mind-blowing in taste. Start making your truffles two days before they're to be eaten so that you don't have to hurry their preparation.

white chocolate and pineapple truffles

PREPARATION TIME 40 MINUTES (PLUS REFRIGERATION TIME) **COOKING TIME** 5 MINUTES **MAKES** 30

¼ cup (60ml) cream

250g white eating chocolate, chopped coarsely

¼ cup (55g) finely chopped glacé pineapple

1 tablespoon Malibu

250g white chocolate Melts, melted

1⅓ cup (100g) shredded coconut, toasted

1 Combine cream and chopped chocolate in small saucepan; stir over low heat until smooth. Stir in pineapple and Malibu. Transfer mixture to small bowl, cover; refrigerate 3 hours or overnight.

2 Working with a quarter of the chocolate mixture at a time (keeping remainder refrigerated), roll rounded teaspoons into balls; place on lined tray. Refrigerate until firm.

3 Working quickly, rolls balls in melted chocolate, then in coconut. Place on lined tray; refrigerate truffles until firm.

rum and raisin truffles

PREPARATION TIME 40 MINUTES (PLUS REFRIGERATION TIME) **COOKING TIME** 5 MINUTES **MAKES** 30

¼ cup (60ml) cream

200g dark eating chocolate, chopped coarsely

¼ cup (40g) finely chopped raisins

1 tablespoon dark rum

250g dark eating chocolate, melted

1 Combine cream and chopped chocolate in small saucepan; stir over low heat until smooth. Stir in raisins and rum. Transfer mixture to small bowl, cover; refrigerate 3 hours or overnight.

2 Working with a quarter of the chocolate mixture at a time (keeping remainder refrigerated), roll rounded teaspoons into balls; place on lined tray. Refrigerate until firm.

3 Working quickly, rolls balls in melted chocolate. Place on lined tray; refrigerate truffles until firm.

mini fruit mince tarts

PREPARATION TIME 30 MINUTES (PLUS REFRIGERATION TIME) COOKING TIME 30 MINUTES MAKES 24

Fruit mince can be kept, refrigerated, for several weeks, stirring every two to three days. This recipe can be made a week ahead.

FRUIT MINCE

⅓ cup (50g) finely chopped dried dates

⅓ cup (55g) dried currants

⅓ cup (55g) chopped raisins

½ cup (80g) sultanas

2 tablespoons finely chopped glacé cherries

1 teaspoon finely grated lemon rind

2 tablespoons dark rum

2 tablespoons chopped pecans

2 tablespoons brown sugar

20g butter

2 teaspoons plum jam

PASTRY

2 cups (300g) plain flour

⅓ cup (55g) icing sugar

150g butter, chopped

1 egg, separated

1 tablespoon cold water

1 tablespoon white sugar

1 Combine ingredients for fruit mince in small saucepan; stir over low heat until sugar is dissolved. Transfer to small bowl; cover, cool.

2 Make pastry.

3 Preheat oven to 180°C/160°C fan-forced.

4 Roll pastry between sheets of baking paper until 3mm thick. Using a 6.5cm plain cutter, cut 24 rounds from pastry for the bases; using a 4.5cm fluted cutter, cut 24 rounds for the tops. Gently press pastry bases into two 12-hole mini muffin pans; fill each with a heaped teaspoon of fruit mince filling.

5 Brush edges of pastry in pan with lightly beaten egg white, cover with pastry tops, pressing edges gently together. Using remaining pastry, cut out 24 stars. Brush tops of tarts with egg white, place a star in centre of each tart; sprinkle with white sugar.

6 Bake tarts about 25 minutes. Stand 5 minutes before turning out. Cool on wire rack.

PASTRY Process sifted flour, sifted icing sugar and butter until crumbly. Add egg yolk and enough water to process to a soft dough. Wrap dough in plastic wrap; refrigerate 30 minutes.

TIP Tarts can be prepared and frozen, unbaked, in their pans, for up to one month. Bake from frozen in a moderate oven about 30 minutes.

gourmet rocky road

**PREPARATION TIME 20 MINUTES
(PLUS REFRIGERATION TIME) MAKES 36 SLICES**

300g toasted marshmallow with coconut,
chopped coarsely

400g turkish delight, chopped coarsely

¼ cup (40g) roasted almonds, chopped coarsely

½ cup (75g) roasted shelled pistachios

450g white eating chocolate, melted

1 Grease two 8cm x 26cm bar cake pans; line base and
sides with baking paper, extending paper 5cm above
long sides.

2 Combine marshmallow, turkish delight and nuts in
large bowl. Working quickly, stir in chocolate; spread
mixture into pans, push mixture down firmly to flatten.
Refrigerate until set then cut as desired.

scottish shortbread

**PREPARATION TIME 20 MINUTES
COOKING TIME 40 MINUTES MAKES 16**

*Shortbread can be made one week ahead and stored
in an airtight container.*

250g butter, chopped

⅓ cup (75g) caster sugar

¼ cup (35g) rice flour

2¼ cups (335g) plain flour

2 tablespoons white sugar

1 Preheat oven to 150°C/130°C fan-forced.

2 Beat butter and caster sugar in medium bowl with
electric mixer until light and fluffy; stir in sifted flours,
in two batches. Knead on floured surface until smooth.

3 Divide mixture in half, shape into two 20cm rounds;
place on two greased oven trays. Mark rounds into
eight wedges, prick with fork, pinch edges; sprinkle
with white sugar.

4 Bake about 40 minutes. Stand 5 minutes then cut
into wedges; cool on trays.

little chocolate Christmas puddings

PREPARATION TIME 40 MINUTES
COOKING TIME 2 MINUTES   MAKES ABOUT 44

This recipe can be made two weeks ahead. Use either bought or left over homemade pudding.

700g plum pudding

250g dark eating chocolate, melted

½ cup (125ml) brandy

½ cup (80g) icing sugar

200g white chocolate Melts

glacé cherries, cut to resemble berries and leaves

1 Crumble pudding into large bowl. Stir in melted chocolate, brandy and sifted icing sugar; mix well.

2 Roll level tablespoons of mixture into balls, place on tray; cover, refrigerate until firm.

3 Melt white chocolate in small heatproof bowl over small saucepan of simmering water. Cool chocolate 10 minutes. Drizzle over puddings to form "custard"; decorate with cherries.

cherries in vodka

PREPARATION TIME 20 MINUTES
COOKING TIME 25 MINUTES   MAKES 1 LITRE (4 CUPS)

The cherries will last indefinitely. Do not allow metal lids to touch the liquid; you can use plastic or glass instead. This recipe is best made four to six weeks ahead of using. Cherries can be served with cream or ice-cream, and the vodka used in mixed drinks, punch or cocktails.

500g fresh cherries, seeded

¾ cup (165g) caster sugar

2 cups (500ml) vodka, approximately

1 Place clean jars on sides in large saucepan; cover completely with hot water. Boil, covered, 20 minutes. Remove jars from water; drain upright on board until dry.

2 Layer cherries and sugar in jars; pour over enough vodka to cover cherries completely. Seal.

3 Stand in cool dark place for at least six weeks before using. Invert jars occasionally to help dissolve the sugar.

craft

alfresco

Our weather makes eating outdoors the perfect way to celebrate Christmas. We've developed a theme using the fresh, cool colours of summer, yellow, white and green. You can use any colour scheme you like, just make sure to follow it all the way through, from gift wrapping to table setting.

✳ menu

drinks	Lime and Mint Spritzer p13
	Watermelon Refresher p14
nibbles	Three Dips p16
starters	Chicken, Basil and Sun-Dried Tomato Terrine p30
mains	Aussie Barbecued Ham p40
	Cold Seafood Platter p51
sides	Tomatoes with Crispy Basil Leaves p77
	The Perfect Potato Salad p78
	Pasta Salad with Garlic Vinaigrette p85
cake	Frozen Chocolate Fruit Cake Pudding p118
dessert	Mini Fruit Mince Tarts p132

decorations

alfresco wreath

1 bundle of 2mm Round
Rattan Core Cane

tape measure

scissors

kitchen string

2 x bundles of raffia

2.5m thin coloured ribbon

flowers/foliage (either fresh
or artificial)

1 Measure and cut the cane into 1m lengths.

2 Arrange the cut lengths into a circular form, about 3cm thick, ensuring the cut ends are evenly scattered around the circle; this gives the wreath its strength and form. Using kitchen string, tie the cane tightly in four places.

3 Unwrap raffia and divide bundles in half. Start wrapping the raffia, in a clockwise direction, around the cane to loosely cover it. When you come to the end of the raffia, tie on another length with a knot and keep wrapping. Hide any loose ends by tucking them under the wrapping.

4 When you've finished wrapping the raffia around the wreath, tie it off, using a knot that can be used to hang the wreath.

5 Wrap the ribbon around the wreath; tie off ribbon at the back of the wreath, tuck loose ends into raffia to hide.

6 Push flowers and foliage into raffia.

NOTE Use any fresh flowers from your garden for your wreath, if you like. Just remember that you will need to spray it lightly with water to keep the flowers looking fresh. A fresh wreath will last only a day, out of hot sunlight, while a wreath made with artificial flowers and foliage will last forever. If you plan to hang your wreath a couple of days before Christmas, using artificial flowers is, obviously, the more practical way to go. Artificial flowers are available from homewares, department and craft stores.

alfresco cards

- purchased pre-made cards or light-weight cardboard
- assortment of ribbons (including bows and decoratively shaped bindings such as flowers)
- clear-drying craft glue
- double-sided sticky tape
- ruler, pencil, scissors
- tapestry needle and thread

1 If using cardboard, cut and fold to the desired size (see note, below).

2 Cut the ribbons into desired lengths. Using the photographs as a guide only, glue or tape the ribbons onto the cards in your desired design.

3 Use the ruler to very lightly draw pencil lines in a triangular (or tree) shape. Use the needle and thread to sew design onto the card.

NOTE If you wish to mail your homemade cards to friends and family, remember to make them in sizes that will fit standard-sized envelopes. Some pre-made cards come with envelopes, however, you will need to buy envelopes for cards that are cut from cardboard. It is a lot easier to address the envelope before putting the card inside.

alfresco

santa sack

1 square metre hessian

matching sewing thread

1 x 160cm drawstring cord/twine

1 Cut out 2 x hessian panels 48cm x 73cm, add at least 2cm for seam allowance as hessian frays easily.

2 Place hessian panels together and measure 10cm down from the top on both sides of the sack. Machine stitch from that point around sides and base. The open section will eventually fold over and become the drawstring section of the sack.

3 Fold top of each panel over 1cm; press. Fold again, so that the top of the panels align with the begining of the sewn sections, pin; machine stitch. This creates the loop for the drawstring.

4 Thread drawstring through opening at top of sack. If using a double drawstring, cut drawstring twine in half and knot at opposite sides. Alternatively, you can use just the one length for a single drawstring.

5 Turn sack right-side out and press.

decorating sacks

APPLIQUE TREE

50cm x 50cm white cotton fabric

water soluble fabric marker

2 skeins white embroidery thread

needle (chenille #24)

tracing paper

1 Using tracing paper, trace around outline of large triangle from the pattern sheet provided. Cut out triangle, pin to front of white fabric; trace shape onto white fabric using a water soluble fabric marker. Cut out fabric shape; pin to front of sack.

2 Using the white embroidery thread, hand-sew the fabric around the raw edges to the hessian with blanket stitch.

EMBROIDERED TREES

water soluble dressmaker's pencil

green embroidery thread

needle (chenille #24)

1 Cut out the small triangle from the pattern sheet provided. Trace four trees onto the bottom centre of the sack using a water soluble fabric marker.

2 Using two or three strands of thread, embroider around the tree in running stitch; use a couple of stitches to form the tree trunk.

EMBROIDERED TREE

water soluble dressmaker's pencil

white embroidery thread

needle (chenille #24)

1 Cut out the small triangle from the pattern sheet provided. Trace onto the bottom centre of the sack using a water soluble fabric marker.

2 Using two or three strands of thread, embroider the tree in satin stitch. The trunk can be either a single or double straight stitch, 2cm in length.

alfresco gift wrapping

selection of different sized boxes
in green, white and lemon

coloured paper

twine

outdoor embellishments such
as twigs, seeds, etc

selection of ribbons

scissors, pinking shears

clear-drying craft glue

double-sided sticky tape

1 Using the photographs as a guide only, position the ribbon, paper, twine, twigs, stems and seeds etc., on the boxes.

2 Once you're happy with the look of your box, tape or glue the decorations to the box (making sure your gift is actually in the box first, before you tape or glue it up).

NOTE Using pinking shears gives the paper a decorative edge. You can buy these from haberdashery and craft stores, although they can be expensive. A cheaper option, and also available from arts and craft stores, are scissors with various edgings used for paper crafts. When cut on paper, these give myriad different decorative edges.

table napkins

purchased napkins

dressmaker's carbon or
water soluble dressmaker's pencil

green embroidery cotton

needle (chenille #24)

1 Using dressmaker's carbon or pencil, trace or draw an outline of a Christmas tree in the corner of each napkin.

2 Using a double strand of cotton, sew small backstitches around the tree outline.

table runner

purchased table runner 40cm wide

dressmaker's carbon or
water soluble dressmaker's pencil

green embroidery cotton

needle (chenille #24)

1 Using dressmaker's carbon or pencil, trace or draw a row of trees at the end of each runner.

2 Using a double strand of cotton, sew small backstitches around the outlines of each tree.

place cards

place cards or light-weight cardboard in stone or white

ruler, scissors and pencil

stone-coloured thread

tapestry needle

1 If using cardboard, cut to the required size.

2 Measure 1cm up from the bottom and 1cm in from each side. Pencil dots at intervals of about 1cm and use as guide to sew long backstitches across the card.

flower centrepiece

large shallow bowl

frangipani blooms

1 Gently remove blooms from stems. Try not to touch the petals with your fingers, as this can turn them brown.

2 Place a little water in the bottom of the bowl; place blooms in bowl. Don't let the water splash the tops of the petals, as this can cause brown spots.

NOTES Don't prepare the flowers until just before your guests arrive.

Use any fresh blooms from your own garden, as long as they're in keeping with your colour scheme.

Blooms are best bought on the day of use. To maintain freshness, don't remove the blooms from the stems until you are ready to prepare and place the centrepiece on the table.

For an added touch, especially if dining in the cool of the evening, float a couple of tea lights in the water of the flower bowl; the effect will be eye-catching in the evening light when the candles are lit.

contemporary

For an easy, yet stylish, Christmas, you can't go wrong with a contemporary setting. With its clean lines and simple elegance, this modern look is inspired by seasonal red, but combined with stone instead of white, and creates a dramatic, yet uncluttered, setting for your table.

✸ menu

drinks	Long Island Iced Tea p12
	Mixed Berry Punch p14
nibbles	Vodka-Cured Gravlax p19
	Barbecued Duck and Ginger Tartlets p22
starters	Quail, Fig and Orange Salad p33
mains	Slow-Roasted Pesto Salmon p56
	Beef with Herb and Walnut Crust p70
sides	Haloumi, Prosciutto and Spinach Salad p77
	White Bean Salad with Coriander, Mint and Lemon Grass p74
	Honey Mustard Glazed Roasted Kumara p81
cake	Little Gift Cakes p128
dessert	Raspberry Toffee Ice-Cream Cake p106

christmas stocking

1 square metre beige or
red-coloured felt material

matching cotton

tracing paper

pencil

1 Using tracing paper, trace the stocking from the pattern sheet provided. Cut traced pattern in two along dotted line, so you have a rectangular piece (collar) and a stocking leg.

2 Cut 2 pieces of fabric for the stocking leg, adding an extra 1.5cm for the seam. Machine stitch right sides of fabric together. Snip seam, especially around curved part of stocking. Turn stocking right side out.

3 Using the rectangular pattern (collar) as a guide, increase collar size so that it measures 62cm x 21cm (double the length and width of the original size); add an extra 1.5cm for the seam allowance. Cut 1 piece of fabric for the collar.

4 Pin collar to stocking; machine stitch in place. Turn collar up; machine stitch short sides together allowing 1.5cm for seam allowance.

5 Turn and pin top edge over 1cm to form hem; machine stitch in place.

6 Fold collar in half; decorate with either rickrack or buttons (see below).

decorating the stocking

NATURAL STOCKING

65cm red rickrack

65cm beige rickrack

matching threads

8 red buttons

needle

1 Machine stitch red and beige rickrack around base of collar.

2 Hand-sew the buttons evenly around the stocking collar.

RED STOCKING

assorted red buttons

matching thread

needle

1 Randomly hand-sew a mixture of buttons all over the stocking collar.

RICKRACK RED STOCKING

70cm red rickrack

matching red buttons

matching thread

needle

1 Hand-sew a line of buttons around the base of the stocking collar.

2 Hand-sew rickrack from the toe to the heel of the stocking.

contemporary cards

purchased pre-made cards or light-weight cardboard in red, white and stone

selection of red and white buttons in various sizes

selection of ribbons

scissors

clear-drying craft glue

1 If using cardboard, cut and fold to the desired size (see note, below).

2 Using the photographs as a guide only, cut ribbons and organise buttons into desired positions on cards.

3 Glue ribbons and buttons in place.

NOTE If you wish to mail your homemade cards to friends and family, remember to make them in sizes that will fit standard-sized envelopes. Some pre-made cards come with envelopes, however, you will need to buy envelopes for cards that are cut from cardboard. It is a lot easier to address the envelope before putting the card inside.

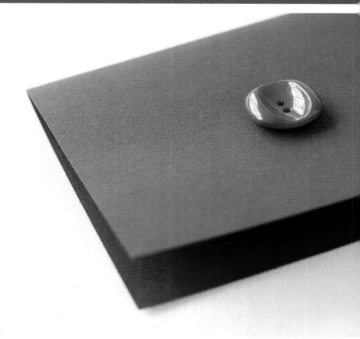

festive tree

1 wire coat hanger
150cm length of beaded wire
small red or white planter pot
small bag of white stones

1 Hold hook of coat hanger in one hand and with the other hand pull the centre of flat-side of coat hanger until both sides of the coat hanger almost come together.

2 Measure 12cm down both sides from where the coat hanger is twisted together and mark position. Bend the wire at these two marks to make a triangle (see opposite).

3 Straighten the hook end slightly, this will help anchor the tree and assist when applying the beading.

4 Starting at the end of the hook, bend the beaded wire around the coat hanger to loosely secure it, then work your way around the whole tree wrapping the beaded clusters to the frame.

5 Put a few stones into the pot then place the hooked end into the pot; add more stones so they fit snugly around the tree, this will secure the tree in the pot.

variations

VINE TREE
1 ball of devil's vine

1 Follow above up to step 3.

2 Wrap vine loosely around hook to secure it, then wrap the vine around the whole tree to cover the wire frame. Tie the vine in a knot to secure.

3 Put a few stones into the pot then place the hooked end into the pot; add more stones so they fit snugly around the tree, this will secure the tree in the pot.

RAFFIA TREE
200g natural raffia

1 Follow above up to step 3.

2 Tie strips of raffia around the hook then tightly wrap raffia around the wire to cover entire frame. Loosely wrap remaining raffia around frame to add thickness and texture to the shape. (If the raffia ends before you have made it back around again, simply tie other pieces to the ends and continue wrapping until you reach the starting point.) Tie off raffia.

3 Put a few stones into the pot, then place the hooked end into the pot; add more stones so they fit snugly around the tree, this will secure the tree in the pot.

gift wrapping

- selection of different sized boxes in red, white and stone
- selection of contrasting fabric
- coloured paper
- craft knife or scalpel
- selection of ribbons and buttons
- scissors or pinking shears
- clear-drying craft glue
- double-sided sticky tape

1 Using the photographs as a guide, position fabric, paper, ribbons and buttons on boxes.

2 Using scalpel, make cuts in box lid, wide enough to thread through ribbon or decorative paper strips.

3 Glue or tape wrapping to boxes to achieve desired effect (making sure your gift is actually in the box first, before you tape or glue it up).

NOTE Using pinking shears gives the paper a decorative edge. You can buy these from haberdashery and craft stores, although they can be expensive. A cheaper option, and also available from arts and craft stores, are scissors with various edgings used for paper crafts. When cut on paper, these give myriad different decorative edges.

placemats

required number of purchased placemats
red buttons in various shapes and sizes
matching sewing thread

1 Randomly sew an assortment of buttons along one side of the placemat, as pictured above.

napkins

4m x 120cm-wide contrasting fabric
(enough for six napkins)
sewing thread to match

1 Cut 6 napkins 60cm x 60cm.

2 To mitre corners, place fabric with main colour facing up; fold edges over 1cm to make hem; press. Fold fabric over 4cm to make border; press. Open out border folds.

3 Fold corner point over 6cm diagonally towards centre of napkin; press firmly. Repeat with remaining corners. Open out corner folds. Turn napkin over.

4 Keeping contrasting colour sides together, fold the fabric diagonally in half so that the two edges meet and the corner forms a point. Stitch across diagonal crease (formed after pressing corner fold in step 3); repeat with remaining corners.

5 Leaving a 5mm seam, cut away fabric bulk. Press seams open; turn corners inside out, press lightly. Machine or top stitch around border to secure to the front of napkin.

NOTE Contrasting fabric can be used either side; if not using a contrasting fabric, start with the fabric wrong-side up and keep right-sides together in step 4.

place cards

purchased place cards or light-weight cardboard in white or stone

red buttons in various shapes and sizes

clear-drying craft glue

1 If using cardboard, cut to the required size.

2 Glue buttons in bottom right hand corner of card to achieve desired effect.

candles

selection of different sized and shaped clear glasses

a variety of semi-transparent paper in various shades of red, white and stone

scissors or craft knife

double-sided sticky tape

ruler

tea lights

1 Cut paper to height of glass.

2 Wrap paper around glass and secure with tape. Place tea lights in glasses.

NOTE If using tall glasses, you will need to buy extra long matches to safely light the candles. These are available from camping stores and supermarkets.

traditional

Whether dining with family or friends, a beautiful Christmas table really sets the mood for a wonderful gathering. White, silver and blue are the traditional cool colours of winter – snow and ice – and, in the heat of summer, anything that suggests cooler weather is a blessing.

✳ menu

sequined place cards

purchased place cards or light-weight cardboard in white

silver sequins

clear-drying craft glue

1 Glue sequins in desired arrangement down right hand side of card.

NOTE Lie card flat while glue is drying to stop the sequins from sliding down the card.

sequined tablecloth

1 purchased tablecloth

enough sequin trim to go around the tablecloth without stretching

1 Pin and tack the trim in place along the edge of the tablecloth, taking care not to stretch the trim.

2 Slip stitch trim to tablecloth.

napkin rings

purchased napkins
1 length silver wire beading
small pliers

1 Roll napkins. Lightly wrap wire around napkin.
2 Using pliers, twist ends of wire beading together to form a ring.

decorated candles

candles in various sizes
silver sequins in various shapes and sizes
clear-drying craft glue

1 Glue sequins onto candles to give your desired effect.
NOTE This will need to be done in sections to stop the sequins from sliding down (and off) the candle while the glue is drying. Lay candle on its side, apply the glue and sequins to one area, then wait until dry before applying glue and sequins to next section of the candle.

✳ christmas tree beaded baubles

bauble

1 x 6cm length wire

5 x 3cm length wire

5 x 2cm length wire

5 x 1cm length wire

random collection of silver, crystal,
dark steel and clear glass beads

1 Using 6cm wire, make a loop (see instructions at
top of page 167) and thread on a collection of 5 beads,
put aside.

2 Using the remaining wires, make up a random series
of bead combinations; start and finish each length of
wire with a tiny loop.

3 Thread the wires, through the tiny loops, onto the
6cm wire.

4 Once all wires have been threaded, tightly twist the
end of the 6cm wire around the base of the 5 beads
to secure.

crystal star

3 x 15cm length wire

6 small blue crystal beads

6 pearl beads

6 round silver beads

6 large blue crystal beads

6 small clear crystal beads

36 tiny silver beads

1 Using a piece of wire, make loop (see instructions at
top of page 167). Thread on beads in the combination,
as pictured, stopping at centre crystal bead (13th bead).
Put aside.

2 Using another piece of wire, make a tiny loop with the
pliers to secure beads and start the bead combination
stopping at tiny silver bead (12th bead). Thread wire
through crystal bead on first wire, pull tight, then finish
the rest of bead combination on second wire. Secure
at end with a tiny loop.

3 Repeat step 2 with remaining wire on other side.

4 Finish the last section of the centre wire with beads,
as pictured. Secure with a tiny loop. Bend wires to form
into star shape.

You will need jewellery wire (26 guage), beads, jewellery pliers, scissors or special wire cutters. The baubles begin with a loop for hanging on the tree. Using approx 2cm of the wire indicated, gently bend in half and twist around wire, making an oval loop.

blue-beaded circles

1 x 35cm length wire

2 tiny silver beads

20 glass beads

20 blue crystal beads

1 Make a loop using the wire (see instructions, above); thread on 3 beads (2 silver and 1 small glass) to form the neck of the bauble.

2 Keeping loop and neck straight turn wire at right angles and begin threading the bead combination of a glass bead followed by a blue bead. Leave ½cm at the end of the wire.

3 Twist the beaded wire to form a smaller circle and secure remaining ½cm wire tightly around base of the neck.

bell

1 x 30cm length wire

1 x 4cm length wire

2 small crystal beads

8 small silver beads

6 small round pearl beads

9 cylindrical pearl beads

6 medium round pearl beads

2 small blue crystal beads

24 glass beads

1 Using 30cm wire, make a loop (see instructions, above) and thread on two small crystal beads.

2 Thread on beads in sequence as pictured, above.

3 Secure by twisting wire end around the base of the crystal beads. Trim excess wire; shape into a bell.

4 Twist one end of the 4cm wire into a small loop; thread on one silver and one blue crystal bead. Thread wire through cylindrical bead at base of bell; finish off with a blue crystal then silver bead. Secure with a tiny loop.

blue 5-point star

1 x 50cm length wire
20 blue beads
24 glass beads
48 tiny silver beads

1 Using wire, make a loop (see instructions at top of page 167) and thread on a combination of 3 glass and 3 silver beads. Bend the wire at right angles and, following pattern pictured above, thread on beads, starting with the smaller glass and silver beads (this enables you to turn the wire at the various points of the star).

2 Once all the beads are threaded according to the pattern, secure by twisting the end of wire around the base of the first 6 beads of bauble. Trim any excess wire.

3 Bend each star point at the centre of the glass/silver bead combinations; shape into a star.

silver drop spiral

1 x 60cm length wire
130 silver beads, approximately
70 glass beads, approximately
1 dark steel bead

1 Using wire, make a loop (see instructions at top of page 167); thread on beads, as pictured above, finishing with the dark steel bead and one silver bead. Secure with a tiny loop. Trim excess wire.

2 Bend wire into a spiral shape.

santa stocking

1 x 26cm length wire

1 x 4cm length wire

36 silver beads

3 blue crystal beads

3 glass beads

1 Using the 26cm wire, make a loop (see instructions at top of page 167) and start threading on all the silver beads. Secure by twisting the end of the wire around the base of the loop at the start of first bead. Trim excess wire.

2 Shape wire into a stocking.

3 Twist 4cm wire tightly between silver beads 5 and 6 (counting from first bead after loop).

4 Thread blue and clear crystals on the 4cm wire and fasten to the other side as in step 3.

traditional tree

1 x 20cm length wire

2 small crystal beads

2 round crystal beads

3 tiny silver beads

36 natural shaped blue beads

1 Bend wire in half, make a loop at the top near bend. Thread both sides of the wire together with a small crystal bead, a silver bead then a round crystal bead.

2 Split wires and thread 18 natural beads on each.

3 Rejoin wires, threading crystal and silver beads on both, as pictured. Secure with a tiny loop after the last crystal bead. Trim excess wire.

4 Shape into a tree.

blue spiral circle

1 x 30cm length wire

3 tiny silver beads

40 blue crystal beads

40 smaller blue crystal beads

1 pearl bead

1 Using wire make a loop (see instructions at top of page 167); thread all the beads according to the pattern pictured above, finishing with a silver, pearl then another silver bead. Twist wire into small loop to secure around last bead.

2 Bend wire into a spiral shape.

snowflake

1 x 12cm length wire

4 x 9cm length wire

4 round clear crystal beads

46 smaller clear crystal beads

8 tiny silver beads

6 small round pearls

3 larger round pearls

4 cylindrical pearls

1 Using 12cm wire, make a loop (see instructions at top of page 167) and start threading bead combination for central wire, stop at middle round pearl (8th bead from top). Put aside.

2 Secure a tiny loop in 9cm wire; thread on 1 silver bead and 7 smaller crystals. Slip this wire through the last bead on the central wire, pull tightly, then finish threading on a further 7 crystal and 1 silver bead. Secure with a tiny loop. Repeat process for the second 9cm crystal wire.

3 Follow step 2 for remaining two wires, threading both with a pearl/crystal combination, as pictured above (all four 9cm wires are threaded through the round pearl on the central wire).

4 Once all wires have been threaded through the central bead and secured, finish off the bead combination for central wire. Secure with a tiny loop. Twist arms into a snowflake shape.

connecting circles

1 x 25cm length wire

1 x 15cm length wire

10 round clear crystal beads

9 blue crystal beads

8 small glass beads

11 tiny silver beads (larger circle)

47 tiny silver beads (smaller circle)

1 small crystal bead

1 Using 25cm wire, make a loop (see instructions at top of page 167) and thread on a crystal and silver bead; bend the wire at right angles and thread on the bead combination for the larger circle, as pictured above. Secure by twisting end around first 2 beads.

2 Secure a tiny loop in 15cm wire; thread on a silver and small crystal bead, then remaining silver beads. Form a circle by twisting beginning and end of wire together under the crystal bead, leaving enough wire free to attach the smaller circle to the larger circle under the loop.

christmas tree

3 x 12cm length wire

2 x 8cm length wire

24 tiny silver beads

34 small glass beads

14 blue crystal beads

10 natural beads

8 round crystal beads

1 large blue crystal bead

1 Using a 12cm wire make a loop (see instructions at top of page 167); thread on 1 silver and 5 glass beads, put aside.

2 Secure a tiny loop in one 8cm wire (top branch) then thread on half the bead combination, as pictured above. Thread this wire through the last 3 glass beads on the central stem (this becomes the second branch). Bend wire out to form second branch; complete pattern and secure with a tiny loop.

3 Repeat step 2 with 8cm wire on the other side, then thread another 6 glass beads onto the central wire.

4 Using the 12cm wires, repeat step 2 to complete the lower branches of the tree. Finish off central wire with two glass, two silver and a blue bead. Secure with a tiny loop.

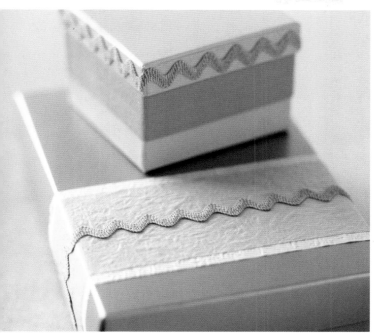

traditional wrapping

selection of different sized boxes
in silver, white and blue

fabric or felt

selection of ribbons
and buttons

coloured paper

scissors, pinking shears

clear-drying craft glue

double-sided sticky tape

1 Using the photographs as a guide only, cut and position fabric, ribbon and paper on the boxes.

2 Once you're happy with the look of your box, tape or glue the decorations to the box (making sure your gift is actually in the box first, before you tape, or glue, it up).

NOTE Using pinking shears gives the paper a decorative edge. You can buy these from haberdashery and craft stores, although they can be expensive. A cheaper option, and also available from arts and craft stores, are scissors with various edgings used for paper crafts. When cut on paper, these give myriad different decorative edges.

traditional stocking

50cm x 120cm main fabric
for stocking leg

25cm piece contrasting fabric
for stocking collar

sewing thread to match

1 Using tracing paper, trace the stocking from the pattern sheet provided. Cut traced pattern in two along dotted line, so you have a rectangular piece (collar) and a stocking leg.

2 Double over main fabric and cut two pieces for the stocking leg, adding an extra 1.5cm for the seam. With right-sides facing, machine stitch around stocking leg. Snip seam, especially around curved areas; press.

3 Using the rectangular pattern (collar) as a guide, increase collar size so that it measures 21cm wide (double the original width); use this to cut 2 pieces from the contrasting fabric, adding an extra 1.5cm for the seam allowance.

4 With right-sides of fabric facing, pin and machine stitch short sides together. Press seams open.

5 Slip collar over stocking, with right sides of collar facing wrong side of stocking and side seams matching. Pin and stitch collar to top of stocking using 1.5cm seam allowance.

6 Fold over bottom edge of collar 1.5cm to form hem; press. Turn stocking right-side out. Fold collar in half and stitch bottom of collar to stocking.

traditional wreath

1 x wreath monkey vine

1 x bundle dodda vine

2 x bunches hydrangeas

1 x bunch assorted foliage in silver and green

catalaya blooms (orchids)

spanish moss

5 x 30cm lengths 18 gauge wire (optional)

1m fishing line

1 Loosely bind the dodda vine around the monkey vine; use wire to hold in place, if necessary.

2 Leaving the stems on the hydrangeas, carefully feed through the wreath, making sure not to break the stems.

3 Repeat step 2 using the silver and green foliage.

4 Using fishing line, simply tie the catalaya orchids into a cluster on the wreath.

5 Finish by placing spanish moss to hide any imperfections.

NOTES The wreath should last up to three days, if sprayed twice daily with water and kept out of hot sunlight.
To save money, you can use the fishing line to tie the dodda vine in place, rather than the 18 gauge wire.
The monkey vine already comes in wreath form from your local florist. Orchids are sold as blooms.

traditional cards

- purchased cards or light-weight cardboard in blue, silver and white
- stencil sheets in Christmas patterns
- paintbrush
- small sponge for paint
- blue and silver paint
- blue, silver and white glitter
- clear-drying craft clue

1 If using cardboard, cut and fold to the desired size (see note, below).

2 Using the photographs as a guide only, stencil designs on cards using paint, or dab stencil area with craft glue and sprinkle with glitter.

NOTE If you wish to mail your homemade cards to friends and family, remember to make them in sizes that will fit standard-sized envelopes. Some pre-made cards come with envelopes, however, you will need to buy envelopes for cards that are cut from cardboard. It is a lot easier to address the envelope before putting the card inside.

glossary

FOOD

ANGOSTURA AROMATIC BITTERS brand-name of a type of aromatic bitters, used mainly in drinks; it is a blend of a reported forty herbs and spices.

APPLE CIDER, SPARKLING unfermented non-alcoholic type of apple juice with sugar added for effervescence.

BACON RASHERS also known as slices of bacon; made from pork side.

BALMAIN BUG shovel-shaped mollusc with flesh similar to that of a lobster. Also known as slipper, shovelnose or southern bay lobster. Substitute scampi, moreton bay bugs or king prawns.

BAMBOO SHOOTS the tender shoots of bamboo plants, available in cans; must be drained and rinsed before use.

BASIL the most common type of basil is sweet basil.
thai also known as horapa; has smallish leaves, purplish stems and a slight aniseed taste. Often used in Thai cooking.

BEETROOT also known as red beets.

BICARBONATE OF SODA also known as baking soda; a mild alkali used as a raising agent in baking.

BREADCRUMBS
fresh bread, usually white, processed into crumbs.
packaged prepared fine-textured but crunchy white breadcrumbs.
stale crumbs made by blending or processing 1- or 2-day-old bread.

BUTTER use salted or unsalted (sweet) butter; 125g equals one stick of butter.

BUTTERMILK sold alongside fresh milk products in supermarkets; despite the implication of its name, it is low in fat.

CACHOUS also known as dragées; tiny, metallic-looking, edible confectionery balls used in cake decorating.

CAPERS the grey-green buds of a warm climate (usually Mediterranean) shrub, sold either dried and salted or pickled in a vinegar brine; tiny young ones, called *baby capers*, are also available.

CAPSICUM also known as pepper or bell pepper. Seeds and membranes should be discarded before use. Also available char-grilled, packed in oil, in jars.

CAYENNE PEPPER *see chilli.*

CHEESE
blue brie soft-ripened, mould-treated cow-milk cheese with a delicate, creamy texture and a rich, sweet taste.
bocconcini from the diminutive of "boccone", meaning mouthful in Italian. Walnut-sized baby mozzarella; a delicate, semi-soft, white cheese.
cream cheese also known as Philly or Philadelphia; a soft cow-milk cheese.
fetta a crumbly goat- or sheep-milk cheese having a sharp, salty taste.
haloumi a firm, cream-coloured sheep-milk cheese; somewhat like a minty, salty fetta in flavour. Can be grilled or fried, briefly, without breaking down. Eat warm, as it becomes tough on cooling.
mascarpone a fresh, cultured-cream product made in much the same way as yogurt. Whitish to creamy yellow in colour, with a soft, creamy, spreadable buttery-rich texture.
parmesan also known as parmigiano; a hard, grainy cow-milk cheese.
ricotta a soft, sweet, moist, white cow-milk cheese with a slightly grainy texture.

CHICKPEAS also called garbanzos, hummus or channa; an irregularly round, sandy-coloured legume.

CHILLI generally the smaller the chilli, the hotter it is. Use rubber gloves when seeding and chopping fresh chillies to prevent burning your skin.
flakes, dried deep-red, dehydrated chilli slices and whole seeds.
cayenne pepper a thin-fleshed, long, extremely hot, dried red chilli, usually purchased ground.
red thai small, medium hot and bright red in colour.
chilli jam a sweet, sourish tangy jam that is sold in jars at supermarkets or Asian food stores. After opening, store it in the refrigerator.

CHINESE BARBECUED DUCK traditionally cooked in special ovens; has a sweet-sticky coating made from soy sauce, sherry, five-spice and hoisin sauce. It is available from Asian food stores.

CHINESE RICE WINE also known as hao hsing or chinese cooking wine, found in Asian food shops; substitute with mirin or sherry.

CHOCOLATE
chocolate Melts ideal for melting and moulding; small discs of compounded milk, white or dark chocolate.
dark eating also known as semi-sweet or luxury chocolate.
Ice Magic a melted chocolate topping that hardens on contact with cold desserts such as ice-cream.
milk most popular eating chocolate; mild and very sweet.
white eating popular eating chocolate.

CHORIZO sausage of Spanish origin, made of coarsely ground pork and highly seasoned with garlic and chilli.

COCOA POWDER also known as unsweetened cocoa.

CORIANDER also known as cilantro, pak chee or chinese parsley; bright-green-leafed herb. Seeds are dried and sold either whole or ground, and neither form tastes like the fresh leaf.

CORNFLOUR also known as cornstarch.

CORNICHON French for gherkin, a very small variety of cucumber.

COUSCOUS a fine, grain-like cereal product made from semolina.

CREAM OF TARTAR the acid ingredient in baking powder.

CREME FRAÎCHE a mature, naturally fermented cream having a velvety texture and slightly tangy, nutty flavour.

CUCUMBER
lebanese short, slender and thin-skinned, with tender, edible skin, tiny, yielding seeds, and a sweet, fresh taste.
telegraph also known as the european or burpless cucumber; slender and long, its thin dark-green skin has shallow ridges running down its length.

CURRANTS, DRIED tiny, almost black raisins; not the same as fresh currants.

DAIRY-FREE MARGARINE commercially made product free of all dairy products.

EGGPLANT also known as aubergine; can also be purchased char-grilled, packed in oil, in jars.

EGGS some recipes in this book call for raw or barely cooked eggs; exercise caution if there is a salmonella problem in your area.

FIVE-SPICE POWDER also known as chinese five-spice; a fragrant mixture of ground cinnamon, cloves, star anise, sichuan pepper and fennel seeds.

FLOUR
cornflour *see cornflour.*
plain also known as all-purpose; unbleached wheat flour.
rice very fine, almost powdery, gluten-free flour; made from ground white rice.
self-raising all-purpose plain flour with baking powder added in the proportion of 1 cup flour to 2 teaspoons baking powder.
soy made from ground soy beans.

GINGER
fresh also known as green or root ginger; the thick gnarled root of a tropical plant.
ground also known as powdered ginger. A flavouring used in puddings and cakes; cannot be substituted for fresh ginger.

GLACÉ FRUIT fruits that have been preserved in sugar syrup.

HARISSA a North African paste made from dried red chillies, garlic, olive oil and caraway seeds. It is available, ready-made, from Middle Eastern food shops and some supermarkets.

JAM also known as preserve or conserve.

KALAMATA OLIVES small, sharp-tasting, brine-cured black olives.

KITCHEN STRING made of a natural product such as cotton or hemp so that it neither affects the flavour of the food it's tied around nor melts when heated.

KUMARA orange-fleshed sweet potato often confused with yam.

LAMINGTON PAN 20cm x 30cm slab cake pan, 3cm deep.

LEMON GRASS also known as takrai, serai or serah. A tall, clumping, lemon-smelling and tasting, sharp-edged aromatic tropical grass.

LETTUCE
cos also known as romaine lettuce; the traditional caesar salad lettuce. Long, with leaves ranging from dark green on the outside to almost white near the core.
mizuna frizzy green salad leaves with a delicate mustard flavour.
radicchio a member of the chicory family with dark burgundy leaves and a strong, bitter flavour.

MAPLE SYRUP distilled from the sap of maple trees. Maple-flavoured syrup or pancake syrup is not an adequate substitute for the real thing.

MARMALADE a preserve, usually based on citrus fruit and its rind.

MARYLAND leg and thigh of poultry still connected in a single piece; bones and skin intact.

MARZIPAN a paste made from ground almonds, sugar and water; sweeter and more pliable than almond paste. Easily rolled into thin sheets to cover cakes.

MINCE also known as ground meat, as in beef, veal, pork, lamb and chicken.

MINI TOASTS very thin-sliced bread, toasted, with the crusts removed.

MIRIN a Japanese champagne-coloured cooking wine, made of glutinous rice and alcohol. It is used expressly for cooking and should not be confused with sake.

MIXED DRIED FRUIT a combination of sultanas, raisins, currants, mixed peel and cherries.

MIXED PEEL candied citrus peel.

MIXED SPICE a classic mixture generally containing caraway, allspice, coriander, cumin, nutmeg and ginger, although cinnamon and other spices can be added. It is used with fruit and in cakes.

MUSLIN inexpensive, undyed, finely woven cotton fabric called for in cooking to strain stocks and sauces; if unavailable, use disposable coffee filter papers.

NUTS, ROASTING nuts can be roasted in the oven to restore their fresh flavour and release their aromatic essential oils. Spread evenly onto an oven tray and roast in a moderate oven for about 5 minutes.

OIL
cooking oil spray we use a cholesterol-free cooking spray made from canola oil.
olive made from ripened olives. *Extra virgin* and *virgin* are the first and second press, respectively, of the olives and are therefore considered the best while *extra light* or *light* is diluted and refers to taste not fat levels.
peanut pressed from ground peanuts; most commonly used oil in Asian cooking because of its high smoke point (is able to handle high heat without burning).

sesame made from roasted, crushed white sesame seeds.
vegetable oils sourced from plants rather than animal fats.

ONIONS
brown and white are interchangeable. Their pungent flesh adds flavour to a vast range of dishes.
green also known as scallion or, incorrectly, shallot; an immature onion picked before the bulb has formed, having a long, bright-green edible stalk.
red also known as spanish, red spanish or bermuda onion; a sweet-flavoured, large, purple-red onion.
shallots also called french shallots, golden shallots or eschalots. Small, elongated, brown-skinned members of the onion family.
spring have crisp, narrow green-leafed tops and a round sweet white bulb; larger than green onions.

PANCETTA an Italian unsmoked bacon; pork belly cured in salt and spices then rolled into a sausage shape and dried.

PAPRIKA ground dried sweet red capsicum (bell pepper); available as hot, mild, sweet and smoked.

PARSLEY, FLAT-LEAF also known as continental parsley or italian parsley.

PEPITAS the pale green kernels of dried pumpkin seeds; they can be bought plain or salted.

POTATOES
kipfler small, finger-shaped with a nutty flavour; great baked and in salads.
pontiac large, red skin, deep eyes, white flesh; good grated, boiled and baked.
sebago white skin, oval; good fried, mashed and baked.

PRAWNS also known as shrimp.

PROSCIUTTO a kind of unsmoked Italian ham; salted, air-cured and aged, it is usually eaten uncooked.

QUAIL small, delicate-flavoured game birds ranging in weight from 250g to 300g; also known as partridge.

RAISINS dried sweet grapes (traditionally muscatel grapes).

READY-ROLLED PUFF PASTRY packaged sheets of frozen puff pastry, available from supermarkets.

RICE

basmati a white, fragrant long-grained rice. It should be washed several times before cooking.

wild not a true member of the rice family but a very dark brown seed of a North American aquatic grass having a distinctively nutty flavour and crunchy, resilient texture.

ROCKET also known as arugula, rugula and rucola; peppery green leaf eaten raw in salads or used in cooking. *Baby rocket* leaves are smaller and less peppery.

RYE BREAD made from 100% rye flour.

SAMBAL OELEK also ulek or olek; Indonesian in origin, this is a salty paste made from ground chillies and vinegar.

SAUCES

char siu a chinese barbecue sauce made from sugar, water, salt, fermented soybean paste, honey, soy sauce, malt syrup and spices. Available from Asian food stores and most supermarkets.

cranberry a packaged product made of cranberries cooked in sugar syrup.

fish also called naam pla or nuoc naam. Made from pulverised salted fermented fish (most often anchovies); has a strong taste and pungent smell, so use according to your taste.

hoisin a thick, sweet and spicy chinese paste made from salted fermented soy beans, onions and garlic.

soy also known as sieu, is made from fermented soy beans.

sweet chilli a comparatively mild, Thai-type sauce made from red chillies, sugar, garlic and vinegar.

Tabasco brand name of an extremely fiery sauce made from vinegar, hot red peppers and salt.

worcestershire a thin, dark-brown spicy sauce used as a seasoning.

SCALLOPS a bivalve mollusc with fluted shell valve; we use scallops that have the coral (roe) attached.

SILVER BEET also known as swiss char, blettes and, incorrectly, spinach.

SPATCHCOCK a small chicken (poussin), no more than 6 weeks old, weighing a maximum 500g. Also, a cooking technique where a small chicken is split open, then flattened and grilled.

SPINACH also known as english spinach and, incorrectly, silver beet. Baby spinach leaves are best eaten raw in salads.

SQUID also known as calamari; a type of mollusc. Buy squid hoods to make preparation and cooking faster.

SUGAR

brown a soft, finely granulated sugar retaining molasses for colour and flavour.

caster also known as superfine or finely granulated table sugar.

icing also known as confectioners' or powdered sugar; has a small amount of cornflour added.

icing, soft ready-to-use cake fondant available in 500g packets and 375g tubs; the tubs are labelled "prepared icing".

palm also known as nam tan pip, jaggery, jawa or gula melaka; made from the sap of the sugar palm tree. Light brown to black in colour and usually sold in rock-hard cakes; substitute with brown sugar if unavailable.

pure icing also known as confectioners' sugar or powdered sugar.

white also known as crystal or granulated table sugar.

SULTANAS dried grapes, also known as golden raisins.

TREACLE thick, dark syrup not unlike molasses; a by-product of sugar refining.

TURKEY BUFFÉ an unboned whole turkey breast with wings attached.

VANILLA

bean dried long, thin pod from a tropical golden orchid; the tiny black seeds inside the bean are used to impart a luscious vanilla flavour in baking and desserts.

extract made by extracting the flavour from the vanilla bean pod; the pods are soaked, usually in alcohol, to capture the authentic flavour.

VIETNAMESE MINT not a mint at all, this narrow-leafed, pungent herb, also known as cambodian mint and laksa leaf (daun laksa), is widely used in many Asian soups and salads.

WITLOF also known as belgian endive; related to and confused with chicory.

ZUCCHINI also known as courgette; small green, yellow or white members of the squash family having edible flowers.

CRAFT

SEWING STITCHES
Start and end all stitches with a knot.

BACKSTITCH
Backstitch is the strongest hand stitch and is used to imitate machine stitches. Bring the needle to the front and make a small backwards stitch through the fabric. Bring the needle through again a little in front of the first stitch, then make another stitch, inserting the needle back at the point where it first come through. All stitches should be of equal length.

BLANKET STITCH
Blanket stitch is a decorative stitch worked around the outer edges of the fabric to create a finished effect. In our project, it is worked at about 1cm apart. Bring the needle through to the front of the fabric at the base of the fabric; next, insert the needle about 1cm up from the fabric base at a 45° angle and, before pulling the thread all the way through, bring the needle up at the base to the front of the fabric again (directly below the insertion point). Take the needle to the front of the thread and pull thread firmly to make a blanket stitch. Keep stitches the same height and width apart.

RUNNING STITCH
This stitch is used for seams, outlines and gathering. Work small stitches by passing the needle in and out of the fabric. Keep the stitches and spaces as even as possible.

SATIN STITCH
This stitch is worked closely together to fill in a solid shape. Work straight stitches, closely together in a single line, across the shape marked on the fabric. Take your stitches to the outside of the line so that the marked line does not show through.

SLIPSTITCH
This stitch is used for holding a folded edge, such as a hem, to a flat piece of fabric. Work with a single thread fastened with a knot hidden inside the hem. Bring the needle out through the folded edge, pick up a few threads of the flat fabric piece and then bring the needle back through the fold again. Slide the needle along and come out of the fold to make the next stitch.

index

index

conversion chart

measures

One Australian metric measuring cup holds approximately 250ml; one Australian metric tablespoon holds 20ml; one Australian metric teaspoon holds 5ml.

The difference between one country's measuring cups and another's is within a two- or three-teaspoon variance, and will not affect your cooking results. North America, New Zealand and the United Kingdom use a 15ml tablespoon.

All cup and spoon measurements are level. The most accurate way of measuring dry ingredients is to weigh them. When measuring liquids, use a clear glass or plastic jug with the metric markings.

We use large eggs with an average weight of 60g.

dry measures

METRIC	IMPERIAL
15g	½oz
30g	1oz
60g	2oz
90g	3oz
125g	4oz (¼lb)
155g	5oz
185g	6oz
220g	7oz
250g	8oz (½lb)
280g	9oz
315g	10oz
345g	11oz
375g	12oz (¾lb)
410g	13oz
440g	14oz
470g	15oz
500g	16oz (1lb)
750g	24oz (1½lb)
1kg	32oz (2lb)

liquid measures

METRIC	IMPERIAL
30ml	1 fluid oz
60ml	2 fluid oz
100ml	3 fluid oz
125ml	4 fluid oz
150ml	5 fluid oz (¼ pint/1 gill)
190ml	6 fluid oz
250ml	8 fluid oz
300ml	10 fluid oz (½ pint)
500ml	16 fluid oz
600ml	20 fluid oz (1 pint)
1000ml (1 litre)	1¾ pints

length measures

METRIC	IMPERIAL
3mm	⅛in
6mm	¼in
1cm	½in
2cm	¾in
2.5cm	1in
5cm	2in
6cm	2½in
8cm	3in
10cm	4in
13cm	5in
15cm	6in
18cm	7in
20cm	8in
23cm	9in
25cm	10in
28cm	11in
30cm	12in (1ft)

oven temperatures

These oven temperatures are only a guide for conventional ovens. For fan-forced ovens, check the manufacturer's manual.

	°C (CELSIUS)	°F (FAHRENHEIT)	GAS MARK
Very slow	120	250	½
Slow	150	275-300	1-2
Moderately slow	160	325	3
Moderate	180	350-375	4-5
Moderately hot	200	400	6
Hot	220	425-450	7-8
Very hot	240	475	9

Senior editor Wendy Bryant
Designer Kasia Froncek
Food editor Elizabeth Macri
Food director Pamela Clark
Special feature photographer Rob Palmer
Special feature stylist Stephanie Souvlis
Special feature food preparation
Elizabeth Macri
Craft consultants Georgina Dolling,
Fiona Roberts
Special feature craft projects
Jo McComiskey, Margaret Stork,
Corey Butler, Judson Bridges

ACP Books
Editorial director Susan Tomnay
Creative director Hieu Chi Nguyen
Director of sales Brian Cearnes
Marketing director Matt Dominello
Marketing manager Bridget Cody
Production manager Cedric Taylor

Chief executive officer Ian Law
Group publisher Pat Ingram
General manager Christine Whiston
Editorial director (WW) Deborah Thomas

WW food team Lyndey Milan,
Alexandra Elliott, Frances Abdallaoui

Cover White chocolate and
pineapple truffles, page 131
Photographer Rob Palmer
Stylist Stephanie Souvlis
Food preparation Elizabeth Macri
Back cover Asian-style baked ham, page 69
Photographer Ian Wallace
Stylist Louise Pickford
Food preparation Elizabeth Macri

Photographers Alan Benson, Steve Brown,
Chris Chen, Joshua Dasey, Ben Dearnley,
Joe Filshie, Louise Lister, Tim Robinson,
Brett Stevens, Ian Wallace, Andrew Young
Stylists Wendy Berecry, Janelle Bloom,
Margot Bradden, Kirsty Cassidy, Marie-Helene
Clauzon, Michaela le Compte, Jane Hann,
Amber Keller, Hieu Nguyen, Sarah O'Brien,
Louise Pickford

Produced by ACP books, Sydney, published by ACP Magazines Ltd.
54 Park St, Sydney NSW Australia 2000. GPO Box 4088, Sydney NSW 2001.
Ph: (02) 9282 8618 Fax: (02) 9267 9438.
www.acpbooks.com.au acpbooks@acpmagazines.com.au
To order books phone 136 116 (within Australia).
Send recipe enquiries to recipeenquiries@acpmagazines.com.au
Printed by Toppan Printing Co., Hong Kong

Rights enquiries Laura Bamford, Director ACP Books. lbamford@acpmedia.co.uk

Australia Distributed by Network Services,GPO Box 4088, Sydney, NSW 1028.
Ph: (02) 9282 8777 Fax: (02) 9264 3278.
networkweb@networkservicescompany.com.au
United Kingdom Distributed by Australian Consolidated Press (UK), Moulton Park Business Centre,
Red House Rd, Moulton Park, Northampton, NN3 6AQ
Ph: (01604) 497 531 Fax: (01604) 497 533 books@acpmedia.co.uk
Canada Distributed by Whitecap Books Ltd, 351 Lynn Ave,
North Vancouver, BC, V7J 2C4 Ph: (604) 980 9852 Fax: (604) 980 8197
customerservice@whitecap.ca www.whitecap.ca
New Zealand Southern Publishers Group, 44 New North Rd,
Eden Terrace, Auckland.
Ph: (64 9) 309 6930 Fax: (64 9) 309 6170 hub@spg.co.nz
South Africa Distributed by PSD Promotions (Pty) Ltd, PO Box 1175,
Isando, 1600, Gauteng, Johannesburg, SA.
Ph: (011) 392 6065 Fax (011) 392 6079 orders@psdprom.co.za

Clark, Pamela.
The Australian Women's Weekly Christmas Food & Craft
Includes index.
ISBN-13 978 1 86396 606 1
ISBN-10 1 86396 606 4
1. Christmas cookery. 2. Handicraft.
I. Title. II. Title: Christmas Food & Craft
III. Title: Australian Women's Weekly

641.5686
© ACP Magazines Ltd 2006
ABN 18 053 273 546

The publishers would like to thank the following for props used in photography:
The Bay Tree, Plenty Homewares, Papaya Homewares, No Chintz, Piggots Store,
Prop Stop, Sirocco Homewares, My Island Home